Modern Mongolia

Modern Mongolia
Reclaiming Genghis Khan

PAULA L.W. SABLOFF, editor

with contributions from
Munhtuya Altangerel
Nasan Dashdendeviin Bumaa
Eliot Grady Bikales and
Paula L.W. Sabloff

University of Pennsylvania Museum of Archaeology and Anthropology
Philadelphia

National Museum of Mongolian History
Ulaanbaatar
2001

Library of Congress Cataloging-in-Publication Data

Modern Mongolia : reclaiming Genghis Khan / Paula L.W.
Sabloff, editor.
        p. cm.
Includes bibliographical references and index.
    ISBN 0-924171-90-1 (alk. paper)
    1. Mongolia—History. I. Sabloff, Paula L.W.
    DS798.75 .M63 2001
    951'.7—dc21
                                            2001004443

Printed in the United States of America on acid-free paper.

Special funding for this book was provided by the Samuel T. Freeman Charitable Trust.

Published on the occasion of *Modern Mongolia: Reclaiming Genghis Khan*, an exhibition organized by the University of Pennsylvania Museum of Archaeology and Anthropology, Philadelphia, in cooperation with the National Museum of Mongolian History, Ulaanbaatar.

Generous contributions to the exhibition came from Ms. Annette Merle-Smith, Mr. and Mrs. Robert M. Baylis, Mr. and Mrs. A. Bruce Mainwaring, Dr. Charles K. Williams II, MGordon Hattersley, Mr. Michael Monier, Mr. and Mrs. Terence C. Golden, Mr. and Mrs. John C. Hover II, Mr. and Mrs. Alvin V. Shoemaker, Ms. Laura Fisher, Mr. and Mrs. Harry C. Kahn II, and Ms. Criswell Gonzales.

The following foundations have also provided support for the exhibition: The Seth Sprague Educational and Charitable Foundation, the Trust for Mutual Understanding, the Hoxie Harrison Smith Foundation, Host Marriott Corporation, the J. Willard and Alice S. Marriott Foundation, the T. Rowe Price Foundation, and the Schuyler Van Rensselaer Cammann Memorial Fund.

PRONUNCIATION CHART

A = ah as in 'lot'
E = eh as in 'let'
I = ih as in 'if'
O = oh as in 'only'
U = oo as in root OR ou as in 'horrible'

This book is dedicated to my husband,

JEREMY ARAC SABLOFF

Contents

The Authors

Munhtuya Altangerel was born and raised in Ulaanbaatar, Mongolia, having graduated from Russian-Mongolian Joint-venture School #3. Ms. Altangerel is a 1999 graduate of the University of Pennsylvania, where she majored in International Relations and wrote her senior honors thesis on Mongolia's status as a buffer state between Russia and China in the twentieth century. She is currently a Master of Science candidate at the Development Studies Institute, London School of Economics.

Eliot Grady Bikales, Assistant Curator, National Museum of Mongolian History, received a master's degree in East Asian Studies from Harvard University and a master's degree in Library and Information Science from Simmons College. While at the National Museum, she has received two grants from the Mongolian Foundation for Open Society, a member of the Soros network, to support the publication of a guidebook on the museums of Ulaanbaatar and to organize a workshop on art handling and preventive conservation. She resides in Ulaanbaatar, where she teaches Mongolian history at the International School.

Nasan Dashdendeviin Bumaa, Curator of Twentieth-century History, National Museum of Mongolian History, received a bachelor's degree from the Voronezh State University of Russia in the former Soviet Union and a Ph.D. from the Institute of History of the Mongolian Academy of Sciences. She worked on the exhibition on twentieth-century Mongolian history and is currently in charge of the renovation of the twentieth-century history gallery. Dr. Bumaa has published in Mongolia and Denmark on a variety of subjects, including Mongolian craft production and the status of Mongolian culture.

Paula L.W. Sabloff is a political anthropologist who has conducted research on Mongolian democracy and market economy since 1996. Her previous research included studies of peasants and land tenure in Mexico as well as patron-client relations in the United States and Mongolia. She earned a bachelor's degree in anthropology from Vassar College and a master's degree and Ph.D. in Anthropology from Brandeis University. Dr. Sabloff is a Senior Research Scientist at the University of Pennsylvania Museum of Archaeology and Anthropology and Adjunct Associate Professor in the University's Department of Anthropology, where she teaches and continues her research on Mongolian political culture.

Foreword

Americans sometimes take for granted the benefits of living in a democracy. Moreover, we often overlook the fact that our democratic institutions strongly influence all aspects of our lives. It is only when we look at other countries around the globe that we see the pervasive influence of democracy on our daily routine, not only in our actions at home and at work but in our material possessions. When we do look at the world with a comparative perspective, it should certainly come as no surprise that peoples like the Mongolians are willing to risk all to achieve democracy–just like the founders of this country more than two hundred years ago.

"Modern Mongolia: Reclaiming Genghis Khan" offers a new understanding of the historical depth of Mongolia's commitment to democracy, which I find both stimulating and gripping. I hope that readers of this book will share my excitement in gaining a glimpse of modern Mongolia and learning about the historical background of the achievement of independence and the rise of democracy in that fascinating country. I believe this book will cause them to reflect on our own democracy–how it affects all aspects of its citizens' lives from their ability to vote in multiparty elections to the tools and goods they use and consume in their daily activities.

Two of the principal missions of the University of Pennsylvania Museum of Archaeology and Anthropology, which I have the good fortune to direct, are to gain new understandings of peoples and cultures through time and space and to make these findings and insights available to students, scholars, and the general public. These twin goals are being reached through the recent research on Mongolian democracy undertaken by Paula L. W. Sabloff, the publication of this vibrant volume, the posting of a special Mongolia section on our award-winning website (*www.upenn.edu/museum*), and the creation of the joint University of Pennsylvania Museum/National Museum of Mongolian History exhibit.

Because "Modern Mongolia: Reclaiming Genghis Khan" so successfully helps us fulfill our 115-year mission, the University of Pennsylvania Museum of Archaeology and Anthropology is pleased to publish this important volume. It also is proud of its collaborative relationship with the National Museum of Mongolian History, which is being realized through the publication of this book. Just as our respective staffs have learned much from each other, I strongly hope that citizens from both our countries will gain new understandings of Mongolian history and democracy from this eminently readable and accessible work.

JEREMY A. SABLOFF
The Williams Director
University of Pennsylvania Museum
of Archaeology and Anthropology
Philadelphia
Spring 2001

Foreword

There was a time when ties between Mongolia and the United States were not close. Now, however, these two very different nations, on opposite sides of the world, separated by thousands of miles, have begun to form strong bonds. Mongolia's transition to democracy in the 1990s was an important factor contributing to this turn-about in Mongolia-United States relations. There is, however, still a long way to go.

If one wishes to comprehend any nation, it is crucial to have knowledge of that nation's history and culture. Without knowledge of the tumultuous events of the last century in Mongolia, it would be difficult to understand contemporary Mongolian society and the goals and dreams of Mongolians today. In my opinion, the driving force behind twentieth-century Mongolian history has been our nation's struggle for freedom and independence.

I am proud to have the opportunity to present the history and culture of modern Mongolia through the exhibition, "Modern Mongolia: Reclaiming Genghis Khan," and this book. These projects, the result of several years of mutual effort, are jointly sponsored by the sister museums, the University of Pennsylvania Museum of Archaeology and Anthropology and the National Museum of Mongolian History. May they contribute to increased knowledge about our nation and country on the part of all people interested in Mongolian history and culture!

I would like to express my deep gratitude to Joe Wolek, Thomas Gillern, Heather Marshall, Munhtuya Altangerel, and especially, to the exhibit's curator, Paula L. W. Sabloff, for her unfailing dedication and professionalism. And I also thank the many people who have generously dedicated their strength and efforts to creating and presenting this exhibition and this book.

I am full of hope that Mongolian-American friendship will continue to grow stronger and deeper as time passes.

BORJIGID SANDUIN IDSHINNOROV
Director
National Museum of Mongolian History
Ulaanbaatar
Spring 2001

Preface and Acknowledgments

Mongolia is a country with a small population and large territory. Just about halfway around the world from the United States, it is thirteen time zones from Philadelphia, my home. About half the people of Mongolia are pastoral nomads, following their sheep, goats, yaks, cows, camels, and horses from one pasture to another in an annual migration cycle. The majority of the people are Buddhist or shamanist or both. On the surface Mongolia could not look more different from the United States.

Aside from curiosity about a people so different from us, why would Americans care about Mongolians? True, there is the romance of Genghis Khan–the story of how one man, a nonliterate nomad at that, conquered the largest territory of anyone in the history of the world. And there is the mystery of pastoral nomads who live so differently from most of us. But there is also a deep-seated connection between the Mongolian and American people, and that is a similarity in our cultural heritage. Both peoples share a love of independence and freedom that are embedded in our democratic governments and capitalist economies. Both nations have linked political culture (independence) and political structure (government) through revolution, the fight against more powerful nations for the right to self-determination and democracy. And both nations achieved this right with help from friends.

The story of nations achieving self-determination and democracy is thrilling and needs to be told over and over. This retelling enforces our own celebration of national freedom and helps us appreciate other nations that have gone through the same struggle as the United States. The story also helps us see the nuances among different nations' adaptations of democratic government and market economy. And it helps us understand the linkage between political culture (how a people believe they should be governed), government, and economy.

This book grew out of my initial exploration of Mongolians' ideas of democracy starting in 1996. While conducting anthropological research in Ulaanbaatar on a related topic, Mongolians' off-hand comments about democracy piqued my curiosity. Did Mongolians use the same definition of democracy as Americans? Political scientists tell us there are over 200 possible definitions, so the Mongolians had many to choose from. But if their definition matches ours, how did this concept catch on so rapidly in a former Soviet satellite? How much of the Mongolian population has bought into this new definition of democracy? And how did the new definition spread so rapidly through the population? I needed to know the answers to these questions.

On that same visit, I met the anthropologists and historians at the National Museum of Mongolian History and we started exploring the idea of presenting a small photographic exhibition on modern Mongolia with a few artifacts at my home museum, the University of Pennsylvania Museum of Archaeology and Anthropology. This exhibition changed and grew over the next four years until it took its present form as "Modern Mongolia: Reclaiming Genghis Khan," a combination of *gers*, dioramas, artifacts, videos, and photographs. This rich combination relates Mongolia's transformation from a feudal, nomadic society under the control of the Manchu Dynasty in China to a literate Communist satellite of the Soviet Union with an emerging industrial sector and finally to an independent democratic nation grounded in capitalist principles and united with the world community.

The exhibition and book share several goals. The first is to introduce Western audiences to the sweep and excitement of twentieth-century Mongolian history that resonates with American history in their similar struggles for independence and democracy. Both countries had to fight twice to secure their present self-determination, the United States in 1776 and 1812 and Mongolia in 1911-21 and 1990. Our project's second purpose is to demonstrate the close relationship between government and daily life by showing how the extreme shifts in Mongolian government affected people's dress, ornamentation, homes, and furnishings. Sometimes we forget how much government does affect our daily lives, and it is good to be reminded of this fact. The third goal is to relate modern Mongolians' national goals to their heritage from Genghis Khan and their nomadic tradition. It is always a shock for people in the West to realize that Genghis Khan, whose rule predates the Magna Carta, affirmed basic democratic principles that continue to guide the Mongolian people, but he did. These chapters, written by two Mongolians and two Americans, together build toward achieving these goals.

Chapter 1, "My Mongolia," is written by Munhtuya (Tuya) Altangerel, born and raised in Mongolia and educated in the United States. I met Tuya when she attended my first lecture on Mongolian history and culture at the University of Pennsylvania Museum. She was a University sophomore, and she was curious to see what I would say about her country. Clearly I passed her test, because we spent the next several years working together. She taught me Mongolian; I supervised her senior thesis. She ate in my home in Philadelphia; I ate in her parents' home in Ulaanbaatar; and we celebrated Tsagaan Sar (Mongolian New Year) in her Philadelphia home. After her graduation, Tuya worked on the exhibition with me for a year before leaving for graduate school in England. Over the course of these years she shared her love of her native land with me, and in this chapter she shares it with the reader, offering not only a broad picture of Mongolia today but also an understanding of her special situation: she completed most of her elementary and secondary schooling under the Communist system, witnessed the Peaceful Revolution of 1990, and now sees her country through the eyes of someone who is aware of Americans viewing her country when she visits her family back home. In the last section of Chapter 1, Tuya briefly reviews Mongolian prehistory and history up to the twentieth century, giving the reader background for understanding Chapter 2, which she translated.

Nasan Dashdendeviin Bumaa (Bumaa), a twentieth-century historian at the National Museum, wrote Chapter 2, "The Twentieth Century: From Domination to Democracy," providing the historical framework for the book and exhibition. Since the demise of the Mongolian Empire, Mongolian history has been influenced by its two neighbors, Russia and China, which have always been uneasy with each other. Over the course of the twentieth century, changes in one or both of its neighbors' situations have triggered serious changes in Mongolia's political, economic, and social organization. This statement does not mean that Mongolia was a passive recipient of outside stimuli. Quite the contrary! Chapter 2 clearly demonstrates the active part that Mongolia took in interpreting and acting upon changes in the neighboring states, always trying to use these external changes to gain independent status for itself along with democratic government and a free-market economy. This trend is clearly seen in Chapter 2 as Dr. Bumaa presents Mongolia's social, political, and economic history in the twentieth century, illustrating it with her own family's story.

Chapter 3, "*Deel, Ger*, and Altar: Continuity and Change in Mongolian Material Culture," shows the strong link between changes in political history and concomitant changes in the material culture of the people of Mongolia, one of the main foci of the exhibition. Using the predominant ethnic group, the Halh, as illustration, Eliot Grady Bikales, Chinese art historian and Assistant Curator at the National Museum of Mongolian History, describes the changes in dress, ornamentation, housing, and *ger* furnishings that accompanied the three changes in government: hierarchical government and feudal society under the Manchu (Chinese) Dynasty, totalitarian government and socialist economy under the Soviet-controlled Communist Party, and democratic government and open, capitalist economy under the 1992 democratic constitution. Chapter 4, "Genghis Khan, Father of Mongolian Democracy," presents some of my own research on Mongolians' concept of democracy. By comparing Genghis Khan's democratic principles with the four pillars of democracy that gird our own American democracy–participatory government, rule by law, equality under the law, and personal freedoms–this chapter shows that the man with the bad reputation in the West actually codified the culture of democracy that is in the heads of Mongolians today. And this concept of democracy looks much like the American definition of democracy. While these ideas may be startling to Western readers, most Mongolians know this already.

We have all worked to make this book as user friendly as possible, integrating our own experience and impressions into the text to make it more personal. The photographs, maps, and other images also bring the text to life. These illustrations were contributed by the project's professional photographer, Joseph Wolek; the National Museum of Mongolian History's photographic archives; the Zanabazar (Fine Arts) Museum in Ulaanbaatar; Bumaa's family photographs; my own field photographs; and those of generous friends, Robert M. Baylis and Stephanie G. Spaulding.

An exhibition project that stretches over five years owes its existence to a great many people. As curator of the exhibition and editor of this volume, it is my pleasure to thank at least some of them publicly. The project started with my anthropological research; therefore first thanks are owed the National Science Foundation and IREX for supporting my 1998 and 1999 research, respectively. The Trust for Mutual Understanding gave us the original support to explore the two museums' collaboration on the exhibition, sponsoring an exchange of personnel in 1999. Many University of Pennsylvania Museum of Archaeology and Anthropology patrons backed the exhibition and work that made this volume possible. They are Annette Merle-Smith, Bruce and Peggy Mainwaring, Charles K. Williams II, Bob and Lois Baylis, Gordon Hattersley, Michael Monier, Terence and Kathleen Golden, John and Jacqui Hover II, Al and Sally Shoemaker, Harry and Joan Kahn II, Laura Fisher, and Cris Gonzalez. Generous support also came from the following foundations: The Seth Sprague Educational and Charitable Foundation, the Hoxie Harrison Smith Foundation, Host Marriott Corporation, the J. Willard and Alice S. Marriott Foundation, the T. Rowe Price Foundation, and the Schuyler Van Rensselaer Camman Memorial Fund. The Samuel T. Freeman Charitable Trust provided special funding for the preparation of the book. The support of these people and foundations is a sign of their generosity and an example of the remarkable work of Leslie Laird Kruhly, former Associate Director for Development and Special Events, and the entire Development Office crew.

The people at both museums–the National Museum of Mongolian History and the University of Pennsylvania Museum of Archaeology and Anthropology–have been a joy to work with. They showed me the creative side of writing and building exhibitions, something new for an academic. And their enthusiasm for my initial idea always improved the project.

Special thanks to my Mongolian colleagues and friends: Borjigid Sanduin Idshinnorov, Director; Uriankhan Dugariin Nansalmaa, Head Curator; and Tseeliin Ayush, Curator of Ethnology. Bumaa, the exhibition's associate curator, deserves accolades for working side by side with me on the entire project. Her focus on detail balanced my attention to the big picture, thus making the volume and exhibition accurate as well as exciting. Eliot Grady Bikales, assistant curator of the exhibition, is really responsible for all of this, for she is the one who brought me to the National Museum in the first place and translated the language and culture of our Mongolian colleagues when I could not do so myself. I not only learned Mongolian history and culture from all of them, I also learned the meaning of Mongolian friendship, for we worked together, sometimes shouted together, but always laughed together.

Other members of the National Museum's staff cheerfully performed all the tasks that make the loan of exhibition materials possible, from the Registrar's Office that found and checked all the objects borrowed and archival photographs copied to the men who removed all the huge plate glass windows to allow us to photograph the National Museum's treasures.

In the United States, I fondly thank Gillian Wakely, Interim Associate Director for Program Education and Exhibits, who has made learning about exhibition preparation enjoyable, and Walda Metcalf, Assistant Director for Publications, whose perspicacity and humor guided this book. Many members of the University of Pennsylvania Museum staff made preparation of the exhibition downright fun; they include but certainly are not limited to Jack Murray, Kevin Lamp, Howard Clemenko, Philip Chase, Pam Kosty, Xiuqin Zhou, and Jenny Wilson. No one thanks the Business

Office, but they have also put up with me an awful lot and taught me so many things that I did not want to know. So, thanks to Alan Waldt and his staff!

Communicating the excitement of a project takes the work of creative and helpful people. In that vein, I would like to thank Joe Wolek, the photographer who took most of the pictures for this volume and the exhibition and also coordinated the 2000 photography/video trip, and Tom Gillern and Heather Marshall of Visual Language, Inc., who filmed and prepared the videos that accompany the exhibition.

Munhtuya Altangerel was really the backbone of the project, for she helped shape it during the critical year of its creation, doing the research to write the initial teaching manual, website, and her own chapter; translating anything we needed from and to Mongolian; and acting as interpreter of her culture as well as her language. Many of her ideas and much of her perspective are embedded in the exhibition. Genevra Murray, an anthropology graduate student at Penn, took over from Tuya just as we were ready to gear the project to our audience rather than our own interests. Knowing nothing about Mongolia, Genevra's intellect and interest enabled her to convert the drafts (of teachers' manual, website, and book) written for ourselves into the form that is interesting to the public.

Thanks also to Enkhtsetseg Purev for helping to translate the videos. Finally, William Honeychurch and Minjin Hashbat took time away from their doctoral dissertations to check our spelling and our archaeological facts. Their work has added to my confidence that the material presented here is accurate and appropriate.

On a personal note, I would like to thank Seth Spaulding who gave me the opportunity to visit Mongolia on a 1994 Citizen's Exchange and thus opened up a whole new world of research and friendships for me. Tsetseglen Aduuchin made the democracy research possible by coordinating the project and befriending me in 1998 and thereafter. Her husband, Bat-erdene Khiad Borjigin, former State Secretary of the Ministry of Science, Technology, Education, and Culture, smoothed the way for the project and as friend provided needed support. Bob and Lois Baylis have been critical to

this project, for they believed in my research and the exhibition from our first meeting in 1996 and demonstrated their support in so many ways–from coordinating the project's fundraising to critiquing our first drafts of the volume's chapters and visiting us in Ulaanbaatar in August-September 2000, when they provided sound advice and needed relief.

Extra special thanks really belong to two men. Brian Hackman of Peterborough, England, stiffened my spine when the obstacles seemed insurmountable but really were not. Our walks and dinners in Ulaanbaatar (where he was working for the World Health Organization and I was doing the democracy research) enriched my stay there immensely. His willingness to learn the anthropological perspective and then incorporate it into his work on maternal mortality inspired me to learn more, share more, and keep my perspective.

The second–but really foremost–man is Jeremy A. Sabloff. In his dual capacity as my husband (of over thirty years–an achievement for our generation!) and Director of the University of Pennsylvania Museum of Archaeology and Anthropology, he supported me through this tremendous learning process. He has always inspired me, for his ability to work calmly with all sorts of people has always been amazing to me. Not only have I loved him over the years, but I have also respected his abilities and learned from him. And that is why I dedicate this volume to him.

It is traditional in prefaces for the author/editor to end by thanking her children for their patience while she fulfills her career duties and ambitions. When I started researching in Mongolia and then working on this project, our children were already becoming young adults, Josh as a college graduate and Lindi as a college freshman. If they learned in the process of this project that they did not need me the way they did as children and that they were really lovable and capable people in their own right, then this project has had an extra bonus. But I think they knew this already. What I hope they also know is that they have always been my top priority–if not in time, then in my thoughts and heart.

PAULA L.W. SABLOFF

Chapter 1

My Mongolia

MUNHTUYA ALTANGEREL

MY COUNTRY IS MONGOLIA, a land of blue skies, wide grass steppes, snow-capped mountains, forested hills, and a golden desert. My people are friendly, hospitable, and proud. We combine our nomadic tradition with a modern lifestyle, riding horses through the wild countryside or hurrying down busy city streets, to catch up with the fast pace of the twenty-first century. I lived all my life in Mongolia until I went to the United States for higher education. I grew to love and appreciate my second home, the country that provided me with the opportunity to widen my horizons, but Mongolia is where my heart is–from where I draw strength and find solace. I am honored to introduce you to my homeland and to share my experience and knowledge of this fascinating land.

Mongolia is an independent nation in the heart of Central Asia, situated between Russia and China. The Mongolian peoples have lived in their present territory since prehistoric times. In the thirteenth century, Mongolia reached its zenith of power and fame when Genghis Khan established the Great Mongolian Empire, the largest empire to exist on the face of the earth under one man's rule. Following a hiatus of several centuries, the Manchu Dynasty of China ruled Mongolia for more than 200 years, from 1691 to 1911. In 1921, Mongolia broke free of foreign rule and declared its independence, only to become a Communist, satellite state of the Soviet Union. In 1990, Mongolia became an independent, democratic nation.

I was born in Ulaanbaatar, the capital city of Mongolia, and lived there until I was eighteen.

Figure 1.1, below. The blue skies of Mongolia are seen on the road to Harhorin. (Joseph Wolek, August 1999)

Map 1, facing above. Mongolia today.

Figure 1.2, facing, below. Nomads of Hentii Aimag herding sheep and goats to a new pasture. (Joseph Wolek, August 2000)

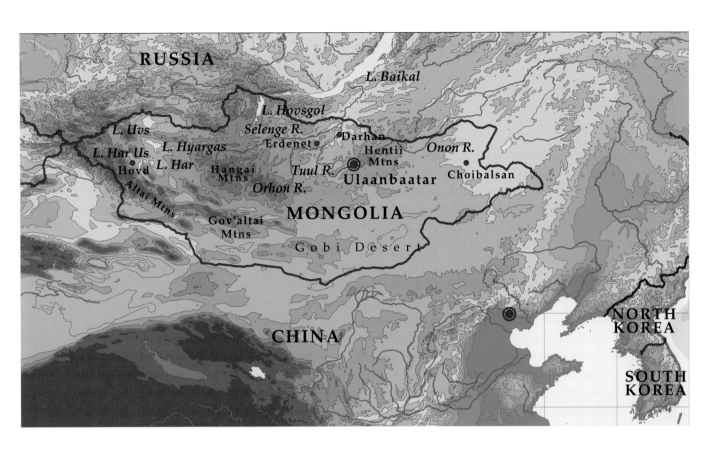

My childhood years were spent under the Communist regime of the late 1970s and '80s when the Soviet Union was our "big brother" and the major contributor to our economy, culture, and education. We wore Russian school uniforms with Lenin buttons bearing the slogan "Always be ready (to fight for communism)." We sang songs about our victory over "stinky capitalism and its followers," praising the international unity of socialist countries.

My teachers instructed us to live and work for the collective good and to forsake all individualistic desires. They taught us why our way was superior and why evil enemies like the United States were destined to fail miserably. We watched Soviet TV and cartoons (they are the best!). As an impressionable teenager, I believed that I was living in a much better society, where people cared for each other and submitted their will to the State and to the Communist Party, where the State took care of our health, education, and living arrangements.

In the late 1980s, as I grew older, I began to sense that my country was becoming agitated and troubled. TV news broadcasts showed long government sessions in which the leaders blamed one another for the senseless purges committed in the 1930s and '40s that killed thousands of intellectuals, religious leaders, and other "enemies of the State." Both the Communist Party officials and the common people were concerned about the artificial economy in which one-third of the national income came directly from the Soviets. *Perestroika* (restructuring) and *glasnost'* (openness), Russian words for the processes of renewing the political structure, building a more open society, and giving more freedom to its citizens, were on everyone's lips.

Figure 1.3. Ulaanbaatar today, showing the three types of housing: The traditional ger of the nomads, a wooden house from the early twentieth century, and a Communist-era apartment building. (Joseph Wolek, August 2000)

I, too, noticed social ailments and injustice: I saw that alcoholism and its devastating consequences touched many Mongolian families, and I saw that everybody was equally poor except for the important Party officials and government bureaucrats. I saw that our supposedly egalitarian society was in fact segregated; most Mongolians were treated as second-class citizens while the Russian specialists and important Party officials had their own luxurious apartment buildings and exclusive stores filled with imported goods. My highly educated parents, one a university professor and the other a medical doctor, received minuscule salaries, and all five of us (my parents, my two brothers, and I) lived in a two-room apartment, with just enough money to buy necessities.

Figure 1.4. While the city is full of eight-story buildings, the suburbs are ger *compounds. (Joseph Wolek, August 2000)*

Figure 1.5. The girl on the left is wearing a Communist-era school uniform for her high school graduation, Darhan. (Paula L.W. Sabloff, June 1994)

Although many remained faithful to the Communist government and performed their jobs with no complaints, there was widespread dissatisfaction. We were supposed to be economically equal under communism, but did that mean we should all be equally poor? And what about political equality? Why couldn't a citizen criticize the government, and why was there no freedom of expression? Why were we so cut off from the rest of the world? Why were our economy and ideology so dependent on one country, Russia? We wanted the personal freedoms and human rights enjoyed by citizens of Western nations; we wanted to freely choose our government; and we wanted to abolish one-party dictatorship. We also wanted to get back in touch with our ancient traditions, drawing ideas from them so that we could develop in a new direction.

With the fall of the Berlin Wall in November 1989 and the crumbling Communist structure behind the entire Iron Curtain, Mongolian citizens became unified in their goal to abolish their Communist regime. In early 1990, underground pro-democracy movements openly urged the citizenry to join them as they held numerous demonstrations and hunger strikes in such places as Suhbaatar Square, Ulaanbaatar, in front of the national Parliament. The demonstrators took great risks as the Communist Party could have used military force against them, although they never did. The demonstrators demanded freedom of speech, free and just elections, a multi-party system, and basic human rights.

As I walked past the demonstrators and hunger strikers in March 1990, I was amazed at the sheer number of people gathered in opposition to the government. The whole giant square, similar to Moscow's Red Square, was full of people of all ages demanding that the Communist government resign, putting aside any fears of possible military intervention. I was only fourteen then, and I remember feeling great excitement even though I did not fully understand the tremendous social transformation our society was undergoing. My friends and I visited the square often to watch for any new developments, happy to skip school and absorb the mass agitation and excitement.

The Mongolian people succeeded in their united effort, and the Communist government

fell in May 1990. At that time, the winds of democracy began blowing over my blue-skied country, and changes began to take place. A multi-party system emerged, and after seventy years of silence and submission, the Mongolian people finally felt they were the real masters of their own lives and land. They chose their government in open elections and expressed their opinions freely; they were no longer afraid of watchful government eyes and purges. Private businesses flourished, and state enterprises became privatized.

However exciting and invigorating, the democratic changes brought about many hardships as well. With the sudden withdrawal of Soviet aid to Mongolia, the country felt as helpless as a baby without a milk bottle. Right after the democratic revolution, the economy nearly collapsed, and we all lived for two years in a state of near starvation. The government rationed milk, bread, meat, and vodka for each family. People stood in long lines from morning 'til evening, often unable to get their daily ration. I remember how my brother would wake up at five o'clock in the morning to stand in line for two loaves of bread. He would return home in the afternoon clutching the loaves, happy that he was able to get them. I often stood in line for my grandmother's meat for eight hours, with my stomach hurting from hunger pangs.

Soon the food troubles were over, and the new government managed to stop rationing basic commodities. Thanks to the business people who imported Chinese and European products and to the Green Revolution which encouraged people to grow their own vegetables, food became plentiful and various. Today, Mongolia is connected to the global economy, exporting to the world market and importing from all over the world. World powers such as Japan and the United States and international organizations and programs such as USAID, the IMF, and the World Bank support the Mongolian democratic process, offering substantial economic aid and advice as Mongolia learns to operate in the capitalist global economy.

Other changes took place rapidly. By 1994, numerous Westerners began to visit my country, eager to find new opportunities for investment (Mongolia was one of the first former Communist nations to try capitalism and

Figure 1.6. Mercury Market, Ulaanbaatar: While the eggs are local, other products come from China, Korea, Italy, and the former Eastern bloc nations. (Paula L.W. Sabloff, June 1994)

democracy simultaneously) and delighted to explore an exotic and remote setting. While many Westerners came to support our democratic development, some came to spread their religious teachings. Mongolia was truly becoming an open country, allowing freedom in all spheres of human activity.

As for myself, I graduated from a joint venture Russian-Mongolian high school in 1994 and decided that learning English was necessary for my further advancement. I enrolled in an English course taught by an American missionary and later found employment with an educational Christian American organization. My experience set my heart to study in an American university. A year later, after passing the TOEFL test and the SATs and with the help of many American friends, I was admitted to the University of Pennsylvania to study for an undergraduate degree. Since Mongolian democratization, other young people have been able to study in Western countries and explore the world of democracy and capitalism that had been inaccessible to us for many decades.

During the years of my American studies, I

returned to Mongolia for summer vacations and noticed more transformations in the country. City streets were filled with new restaurants selling international cuisine. New build-

Figure 1.7. Modern advertising in Ulaanbaatar is in English, Mongolian, or sometimes the Mongolian language written in English letters. (Joseph Wolek, September 2000)

ings emerged everywhere, and private housing became a new fancy of rich business people (before, everyone had lived in large apartment blocks). Big companies displayed their advertisements on billboards, and new small businesses opened practically every day. Giant modern supermarkets became commonplace, and Japanese SUV's and German BMW's caused traffic jams in the central city. Ulaanbaatar as well as popular nature spots were flooded with international tourists. Recently I noticed that during the national celebration of Naadam,[1] Mongolia's independence day, foreign visitors filled half of the stadium! In the countryside, herders were now raising private herds of cattle and selling cashmere to Mongolian or Chinese merchants. Tourist companies had set white *ger*s in rows to beckon weary travelers to relax and enjoy the clear summer nights.

This is how modern Mongolia looks to me. I give below a more extensive account of Mongolian geography. Frankly, it is difficult to describe the geography of a nation with such a vast territory as Mongolia.

Figure 1.8. Tourist gers in a row, waiting for customers, Tuv Aimag. (Joseph Wolek, September 2000)

Geography

Compared with its two gigantic neighbors, China and Russia, Mongolia seems diminutive in size, but it has a total area of 971,913 square miles (1,564,100 square km). If placed inside United States borders, Mongolia would stretch from Washington DC to Denver (see Map 2).

Extending from the Siberian tundra down to the heart of the Gobi Desert, Mongolia has a strikingly diverse landscape. Mountains and hills occupy over 40 percent of Mongolian territory. The Mongolian Altai, the longest and highest mountain chain, covers a good part of western Mongolia as it stretches north to south. It contains many snow-capped peaks, including Huiten (cold) Peak (15,272 feet, 4,653m), the highest point in Mongolia. The Mongolian Altai has over 200 glaciers.

I have been to the edge of the Altai Mountains whose mystical summits are eternally covered with snow and hidden in the clouds. This is where the snow leopards, one of the rare and endangered species in the world, live, and how I wished to see one!

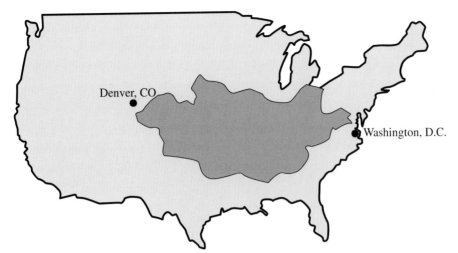

Map 2. Mongolia's size compared with the United States.

Figure 1.9.
A Golden eagle perches on the arm of an eagle hunter, Bayan Olgii Aimag. (Robert M. Baylis, August 2000)

Figure 1.10, facing. Herding yaks in the Altai mountain range, Bayan Olgii Aimag. (Robert M. Baylis, August 2000)

Wild sheep and golden eagles are two other exotic high mountain inhabitants. The former have long horns that twist into a circle and become very heavy with age. The old wild sheep are known for climbing up to the highest mountain peak and plunging to their deaths.

My parents and grandparents came from the western aimag (province) of Hovd (Khovd)* and lived on the banks of Lake Har Us (Black Water). My grandmother used to tell me a story she had heard as a child, of how Lake Har Us was said to be inhabited by giant creatures (much like the Loch-Ness monster) that lurked in the still dark waters and around the dense vegetation of the lakeshore. Children were told not to swim far from shore lest they be caught by the monsters. One of these days I plan to explore this beautiful region of rocks, mountains, and mystical lakes where my kin lived before they moved to the city.

The Gov' Altai mountain chain runs through the Gobi Desert in southern Mongolia, and its rocky, snow-peaked mountains juxtaposed against the yellow sand of the desert create magnificent scenery. The Gov' Altai Mountains are also home to snow leopards.

The Gobi covers one-third of Mongolia.[2] I have visited the sand dunes of the northern Gobi, where I played in its golden sand, rode on a two-humped camel (it spat in my friend's face!) and tried to catch slippery lizards. But most of the Gobi consists of rocky deserts and

Figure 1.11, facing below. Yaks at the Hovd River, Hovd. (Paula L.W. Sabloff, July 1998)

Figure 1.12, below. The Gobi Desert on the road to Harhorin. (Stephanie G. Spaulding, June 1994)

* The spelling in parentheses is the old way of spelling the preceding word.

Figure 1.13, facing. Erdene Zuu Monastery near the site of Harhorin, Genghis Khan's city. (Stephanie G. Spaulding, June 1994)

small oases with tall green grass and leafy trees; only a small part of the Gobi has sandy dunes.

The dinosaur graveyard, where paleontologists discovered a rich collection of intact skeletons and dinosaur eggs, is also found in the Gobi.[3] The desert steppe and Gobi desert zones have many modern exotic inhabitants such as desert bears, or *mazaalai*, and red wolves. Herds of fast gazelles and antelopes sweep through the Gobi while wild asses and camels maintain a foothold in their native habitat.

On the central steppes covered with green pastures stretching toward the horizon, rivers shaped like silver snakes glistening in the sunlight cut through the valleys. This is where Genghis Khan's magnificent capital Harhorin (Karakorum) once rose in glory, welcoming traders and emissaries from foreign lands at the city gates. The forest steppe animals include red deer, sables, muskrats, fox, steppe fox, and wolves.[4] Typical steppe inhabitants are marmots, wild cats, falcons, and steppe eagles. Mongolian nomads hunt marmots for their meat and fur. Przewalski horses (wild horses) used to inhabit the steppe and desert zones. At one point they had become extinct in Mongolia; however a small group were reintroduced into their native habitat from a Dutch wildlife preserve.

In central Mongolia, only twenty minutes from the capital, is Terelj National Park, my family's favorite place to relax and enjoy the fresh country air. The granite rock formations in the shapes of a turtle, camel, and thinking man are fun to climb, and from the top of the mountains you can view the green Tuul Valley where the river flows and tumbles against stones.

We visit our distant relatives in Terelj. They raise cattle and horses, some of which are trained for racing. Our seven-year-old cousin once won the district horse race and was awarded a golden medal, which he proudly displayed to us, a broad smile on his sun-kissed, bright-eyed face. Our kin allow us to ride the horses, and we gallop through meadows bright with steppe flowers, the sound of rushing wind in our ears. Our carefree spirits rise within us and fill us with happiness and gratitude for this beautiful land.

Figure 1.14. A rock formation resembles a giant wave in Terelj National Park, Tuv Aimag. (Paula L.W. Sabloff, May 2001)

In the east, I have roamed through the

Figure 1.16. A Buriad family working in the garden outside their log cabin, Binder, Hentii Aimag. (Joseph Wolek, August 2000)

never-ending rolling hills where hairy, bushy-tailed yaks chew on green grass and bathe in the Onon River. This region is part of the steppe zone that stretches all the way west to the Basin of Great Lakes. The steppe zone is the major pasture area of Mongolia, with grass, shrubs, and blooming plants in the spring. This is the home of the Buriad Mongols, who live in log cabins just as their Siberian cousins do.

Mongolia's major rivers–the Orhon, Tuul, and Selenge–flow on a vast plain in northern Mongolia. The rivers deposit fertile soils used for growing vegetables and grain and green pastures for cattle. The most famous feature of the northern region is Lake Hovsgol, the deepest freshwater lake in Central Asia (873 feet, 266m deep).[5] It is extremely transparent (visitors can see 82 feet below the surface). Lofty

peaks that resemble the Swiss Alps surround Hovsgol, a major tourist attraction, and its dense forests are home to rare and even unidentified plants. Hovsgol is also known for its reindeer, which the Reindeer People (the *Tsaatan* or *Caatan* people) domesticated long ago, relying on this animal for food, clothing, and transportation. I have visited Lake Hovsgol and the Selenge River where stately evergreen trees share land with people who live in Russian-style wooden houses.

However beautiful, the inland location and inhospitable climatic conditions make Mongolia a challenging environment to inhabit. The country has a sharp Continental climate, marked by high fluctuations in daily temperatures and constant Siberian winds. The average summer temperature is only 64°F (18°C), while the average winter temperature is -6°F (21°C)! But most of the days are sunny (about 260 days a year), the deep blue sky with white patches of clouds arching above the land.[6]

Figure 1.17. A Tsataan girl on a reindeer, north of Lake Hovsgol. (Robert M. Baylis, August 2000)

Figure 1.18, above. Tuv Aimag races: as the winner prepares to cross the finish line, her adult escort raises the blue hadag *of victory. (Paula L.W. Sabloff, August 2000)*
Figure 1.19, below left.Tuv Aimag Naadam archery contest: a woman contestant raises her bow, the same construction used in Genghis Khan's day, and prepares to shoot. (Joseph Wolek, August 2000)
Figure 1.20, below right. A Mongolian wrestler and his friend, Tuv Aimag Naadam festival. (Joseph Wolek, August 2000)

That is why my country is called the Land of the Blue Sky.

The Mongolian People

Modern Mongolia is one of the most sparsely populated countries in the world. The population of about 2.4 million people (as of 1999) is distributed over the landscape at four persons per square mile (or two per square km). Mongolia is also a very young country, with over a third of the population fifteen years old or younger and only 4 percent sixty-five or older.[7]

The Mongolian population is relatively homogenous, consisting of peoples belonging to Mongolian and Turkic nationalities: more than 70 percent of the total population are Halh (Khalkha) Mongols, and 24 percent are members of other Mongolian ethnic groups such as Buriad (Buryat), Dorvod, Barga, Darhad, Oold, and Torguud. The remaining 6 percent are ethnically Turkic peoples: Kazakhs, Tuvinians, Urianhai, and Hotons.[8] My father is Halh and my mother is of Mongolian Turkic origin. Many people marry across groups, although Kazakhs usually tend to stay separate. Children belong to the ethnic group of their father.

During Communist rule, people dropped their family names, and until 2000 we were called only by our first names. In place of last names, we used our father's first name. Thus I was known as Altangerel's Tuya. In 2000 the government decided that we should restore

Figure 1.21. Kazakh men in their ger, *Bayan Olgii Aimag. (Robert M. Baylis, August 2000)*

our historical tribal names as our surnames. But many families, especially in the urban centers, had forgotten their tribal affiliation. It is no wonder, then, that more than half of the population claimed they belonged to the Borjigin, the clan of Genghis Khan. My family determined that we belong to the Olhon (Olkhon), a minor tribe in western Mongolia. So my father changed his name to Altangerel Olhon. I, however, have decided to keep the name I used on my American university application: Munhtuya Altangerel. Tuya is my nickname.

The majority of Mongolians practice Tibetan Buddhism, although there is a significant number of atheists resulting from sixty-six years of Communist rule (1924-1990). The Communist government suppressed and persecuted religion severely, destroying more than 90 percent of the country's Buddhist temples and shrines and killing or purging the Buddhist monks. However, the monks' religious influence remained in the hearts of the people, and when the Communist regime disintegrated in 1990, the majority of Mongolians revived their practice of Tibetan Buddhism. Some even returned to the ancient practice of shamanism. The Turkic Mongols, who are usually found in the western aimags, openly practiced Islam. My father, who is still a member of the Communist Party, is an atheist; my mother is a Buddhist. My grandmother prays to the mountains and the blue sky, just as Genghis Khan did.

Today, Christianity and other religions also have their share of followers, usually among the younger generation. But the fascination of Mongolian youths with the Mormons and other Christian sects tends to last for only a short time.

Despite Monglia's disparate religious beliefs, Mongolians from all over the country celebrate Naadam, an ancient festival, with wrestling, archery, and horse races. The national holiday is celebrated July 11-13 to commemorate Mongolia's 1921 liberation from China, but Mongols engage in these Three Sports of Men throughout the year (although they are called the Three Sports of Men, women and children participate as well).

Most of the Mongolian population still follows the traditional nomadic lifestyle, raising cattle in the countryside, moving from one pastureland to the next in an annual cycle called transhumance. They live in felt *ger*s, or yurts, round canvas-and-felt houses with wooden lattice walls that collapse for quick disassembly and expand for assembly in the

Figure 1.24. A typical Mongolian ger, Tuv Aimag. (Joseph Wolek, August 2000)

Figure 1.25. A man reading in the Ulaanbaatar Black Market. (Joseph Wolek, August 2000)

next location. Although 49 percent of Mongolians now live in urban centers,[9] most spend at least some of their summers visiting kin in the countryside and participating in nomadic life. City children often live with their country kin during summer vacations, working on the skills needed to survive as nomadic herders. Virtually everybody can ride a horse and enjoy the traditional nomadic meat-and-dairy diet, including the national drink of *airag*, fermented mare's milk.

Almost half of the population engages in agricultural and animal husbandry activities, roughly one-fourth in trade and industry, and the rest in other sectors such as service, government, education, and science.[10]

Mongolians are highly educated, with programs ranging from nursery school and kindergarten through the Ph.D. and professional schools. The D.Sc. (Doctor of Science), earned above the Ph.D., is awarded in some universities. It should be noted that Mongolian women compose the majority of university students, although there are still plenty of young men who are eagerly pursuing higher education. Today the literacy rate is close to 83 percent, not as high as it was during Communist rule because as some herders prefer to keep their children with them rather than attend local schools.[11]

The capital city of Ulaanbaatar is located in Tuv Aimag in the middle of Mongolia. The seat of national government and industry as well as the starting point for international support programs, Ulaanbaatar is a cosmopolitan city. Tourist books can describe the cultural, economic, and political facts of the city. I want to write about the youth.

During the school season (September to June), the streets of Ulaanbaatar are filled with energetic young people walking to their schools, universities, and jobs. They are very fashionable, wearing the latest styles of Western clothing and taking great care with their appearance. Urban youth are generally very open-minded, combining Mongolian and Western cultures. They listen to the latest international hits and spend a lot of time on the Internet. Internet cafes are spreading across the city like mushrooms after rain, and they are usually crowded with young people.

Today's Ulaanbaatar has changed significantly from Communist times, usually in response to the popular demands of youth.

Figure 1.26. A youth hamming for the camera in the Ulaanbaatar Black Market, near the bicycle sales. (Joseph Wolek, September 2000)

The streets of modern Ulaanbaatar are filled with bars and international restaurants. Disco clubs and karaoke bars are taking over the city. During Communist times, the city looked austere, with no entertainment centers. The only major place for youth to congregate was the Young Pioneers Palace, where children not only imbibed Communist propaganda but also were involved in activities such as singing, drawing, dancing, studying science, and playing sports.

Ulaanbaatar and smaller urban centers have inherited the Soviet-style cement apartment blocks that lack architectural distinction and color. The difference is that whereas under communism the state owned the buildings, today the families that occupied the apartments at the demise of communism have gained ownership of their own apartments. Nowadays families may sell or rent their apartments. Many with first-floor apartments build private street entrances and open shops in their former living quarters. But from an aesthetic perspective, glass skyscrapers, modern European buildings, and Tibetan-style monasteries and pagodas now alleviate the monotony of Soviet-style bricks and cement. This rich mixture of architectural styles gives Ulaanbaatar its special appearance.

Not all Mongolians live in Ulaanbaatar. In fact, not all Mongolians live in Mongolia. They are spread throughout the world, attending universities or working abroad, exploring parts of the world that once were closed to them by the iron curtain of communism.

The Story of Mongolia Up to 1900

Mongolia's story is both rich and tumultuous. For 1600 years, from the Hunnu Empire in the 4th century through Genghis Khan's great con-

Figure 1.27. Soviet-style apartment buildings in Ulaanbaatar were uniform and dreary. (Joseph Wolek, September 2000)

Figure 1.28. A private dental clinic in a former first-story apartment illustrates the conversion of living quarters to capitalist ventures. (Joseph Wolek, August 2000)

struction of the largest empire in the world in 1206, the ancient and medieval history of Mongolia was full of nomadic wars and conquests. From the seventeenth to the twentieth century, my country survived and preserved its culture despite the often-harsh foreign rule of the Manchu Dynasty of China. In the twentieth century, Mongolia became the second Communist country after Russia.

You can see why one could not possibly fit the details of such abundant historical experience into a few pages. However, I will give you a very brief account of Mongolia's story, which I learned from informal schooling provided by private teachers, my parents, and my years of study in the United States–not from my Russian school, which taught me little of Mongolian history.

This brief description might leave the impression that my people's history is best described by the word 'chaotic,' but please keep in mind that these few pages are summarizing more than 40,000 years of prehistory and 2,000 years of history.

PREHISTORY

In the Mesozoic Era (248-65 million years ago) Mongolian territory was once inhabited by giant dinosaurs that roamed the prehistoric landscape. The dinosaurs' remnants are plentiful in the Gobi Desert, which is why Mongolia is sometimes called a dinosaur graveyard.

Archaeologists have found evidence for human occupation of Mongolia starting in the Lower Paleolithic (perhaps 500,000 years ago).[12] These early inhabitants were forest dwellers. With the coming of the Bronze and Iron Ages, Mongolia's ancestors became skilled in the production of bronze tools and more advanced techniques of animal husbandry.

FIRST EMPIRES

Mongolia before Genghis Khan followed a typical pattern of nomadic peoples, alternating

Map 3. The Hunuu Empire (4th century BCE to 1st century CE).

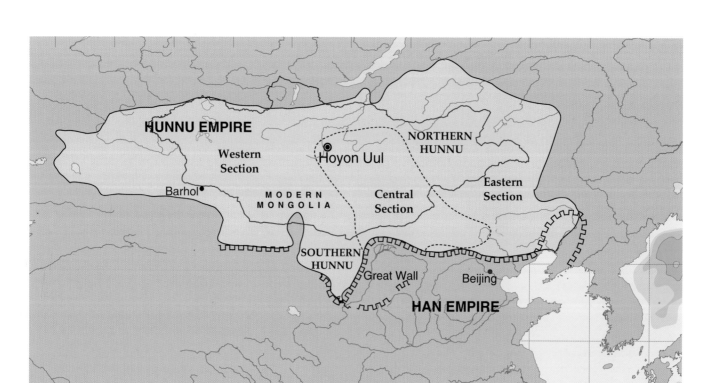

Figure 1.29. Hunnu pottery in the NMMH collection, 3rd century BCE - 1st century CE. (NMMH)

between vast empires and small-scale tribal organization. The first empire on Mongolian soil was the Hunnu (Xiongnu in Chinese) which began in the fifth to fourth century BCE. Society was organized around such economic pursuits as nomadic cattle-raising, agriculture (after the first century BCE), and trading and warring with its sedentary neighbors. This was the period when the Chinese built long walls against northern marauders, as the agricultural Chinese hoped to prevent the nomadic Hunnu from attacking their lands.

The pattern of consolidating local nomadic peoples into one empire and then trading with and raiding southern agricultural groups repeated over the next thousand years.

The Hunnu Empire began to break apart by 53-55 BCE, but sections of the old empire maintained control of Mongolian territory until 93 CE, when an ancient Mongolian nomadic tribe–a segment of the Dunhu people–rose up and vanquished its former rulers. This tribe eventually formed the Xianbei State, which controlled the area until the middle of the third century CE. It was fol-

lowed by two more Mongol states, the Toba and Jujan states.

The Altai Turks defeated the Jujan State in 553. Different Turkic peoples, who originated in Central Asia and migrated to present-day Turkey from there, ruled the Mongolian territory for almost five centuries. From time to time the major Mongolian tribes united under central leadership, but this usually lasted only a short time.[13]

By the middle of the twelfth century, the Mongolian nomadic tribes were surrounded by large empires and encroaching peoples–the Chin Dynasty to the south and east, the Altan people to the east, the Naiman to the west, and the Taichuid to the north. Some of the Mongols had united under the leadership of Habul, great-grandfather of Genghis Khan, but their organization did not last beyond 1160.[14] The Mongolian people suffered tremendously as the economy and the tribal system collapsed from constant internal feuds and external wars, and the population sank into poverty, living in a state of uncertainty, terror, and fear of invasion or assault.

GENGHIS KHAN AND THE GREAT MONGOLIAN EMPIRE

During the time of disintegration and degeneration, Genghis Khan (1162-1227) emerged.[15] He united all the Mongolian tribes into a Great Mongolian Empire in 1206, preventing them from becoming swallowed up by neighboring rulers. Temujin (his childhood name) was born unto a sub-clan of a major Borjigin tribe on the Mongolian steppes. He survived many hardships and troubles in his youth. The Tatars murdered his father, the clan chief, when he was nine years old, and the clan then deserted him along with his mother and siblings. From early on he showed charismatic leadership qualities that enabled him to form a group of faithful followers and arrange important alliances with various tribal chiefs. These chiefs later helped him succeed in his campaigns to reclaim his tribe and unite the Mongolian tribes.

Genghis Khan reorganized the tribes into a military state, dividing the military-age men into units of tens, hundreds, and thousands. Their families were then attached to these military units. Although this system was borrowed from previous nomadic states, Genghis Khan introduced strong discipline, written law, and order. He promoted education (literacy) and knowledge, and encouraged economic prosperity for all citizens. His great military state structure, unity of goals, and support of the people enabled him and his descendents to

Figure 1.30. A portrait of Genghis Khan commisioned by the Chinese after his death. Mongolians believe he looks very sinofied here. (NMMH copy of a painting in the National Palace Museum, Taipei, Taiwan, Republic of China)

successfully campaign against and conquer other nations. That is why his descendants call him the "Father of all Mongols" and credit him with the existence of a free and independent Mongolia today.

By the time of his death in 1227, Genghis Khan had conquered territory from China to the Caspian Sea. His descendants extended the empire from the Black Sea to the Korean Peninsula, incorporating Russian princedoms, Bulgar principalities, Middle Eastern and Central Asian territories, China, and all of East Asia.[16] His grandson Kubilai (Hubilai) Khan established the Yuan Dynasty in China, mov-

ing the Mongolian capital from Harhorin in Mongolia to Dadu (later called Beijing) in China. Another grandson, Batu Khan, leading the Golden Horde, was responsible for vast conquests in the West (Hungary, Bulgaria, Russia), Central Asia, and the Middle East (Iran, Iraq, Armenia, Upper Mesopotamia). The Ilkhanates of the Middle East and India established rule over the highly civilized nations of Iran, Iraq, Mesopotamia, and Persia.

Conquered territories had to pay tribute to the Mongolian khans and endured many hardships from the Mongolian conquests, such as burned and destroyed cities, heavy taxation,

Map 4. The Great Mongolian Empire (13th century CE).

Mongolia when Temujin was named Genghis Khan, 1206

Mongol Empire at the death of Genghis Khan, 1227

Empire at the end of the 13th century

and forced labor. However, the Mongolian Empire brought positive effects as well. The great expanse of the empire allowed trade and travel to flourish between different countries, securing peace along the famous Silk Roads and other trade routes throughout the vast Eurasian continent. The Mongolian capital Harhorin, built during the rule of Genghis Khan's son Ogedei around 1235, had a metropolitan culture, serving as a center of trade, an exchange point of arts and sciences from many cultures, and a religious haven for people of many faiths such as Nestorian Christians and Buddhists. The Mongolian Empire brought together Western and Eastern cultures, thus allowing them to intertwine.[17]

Figure 1.31. Poor, barefoot children in Ih Huree (later called Ulaanbaatar). (NMMH 1917)

MONGOLIA UNDER THE MANCHURIAN EMPIRE

Within 200 years of Genghis Khan's death, the Great Empire began to disintegrate, as nomadic confederations tend to do. In addition to facing difficulties in keeping peace in such a huge territory, disunity among the khans (Genghis Khan's heirs) and the steady resistance of local populations hastened the empire's dissolution. In China, the Yuan Empire of Mongols lasted only 104 years (1264-1368); the great Ilkhanate of the Middle East lasted until the 1330s; and the Golden Horde in Europe dissolved by the middle of the fifteenth century.[18] Three centuries of feuds, the division of the Mongolian land into princedoms, and constant power struggles over the control of the original Mongolian empire followed.

In the early seventeenth century, the Manchus, nomadic people from northwest China, wrested power from the Ming Dynasty of China and established the Qing Dynasty in 1636.[19] Soon after this event, the Manchus began to incorporate disjointed Mongolian princedoms one by one into the Qing Dynasty until 1691, when the Manchu Dynasty ruled

over greater Mongolia. The Mongols continuously sought to gain independence, staging numerous uprisings at the local and national levels. But they could not rid themselves of Manchu oppression for 275 years.

The Manchu rulers employed several strategies to keep the Mongols weak, disjointed, and isolated both from each other and other nations. Perhaps the most insidious was Manchu encouragement of a Tibetan Buddhist hierarchy that imposed various religious taxes on top of the heavy tributes already levied by the Manchu government on an impoverished population. By the end of the nineteenth century, Mongolia was thoroughly isolated, backward, malnourished, and desperate for independence–for freedom from the Manchu Dynasty and from the feudalistic social order.

This volume tells the story of how my people arose from such extreme poverty to proudly join the international community as an independent, democratic nation. Mongolia is an active participant in the United Nations and other international organizations; engages in international trade as exporter and importer; maintains official ties with nations all over the globe; and not only sends her students abroad but also educates foreign students at home to further these ties. My education is a good example of how Mongolia has changed over the century.

NOTES

1. Naadam is celebrated July 11-13 to commemorate Mongolia's 1921 liberation from China. However, Naadam is actually an ancient celebration, with wrestling matches, archery contests, and horse races.

2. Alan J. K. Sanders, *Mongolia: Politics, Economics and Society* (London: Frances Pinter, 1987), 3.

3. Academy of Sciences MPR, *Information Mongolia* (Oxford: Pergamon, 1990), 14.

4. Sanders, *Mongolia: Politics, Economics and Society,* 2.

5. Academy of Sciences MPR, *Information Mongolia*, 30.

6. National Statistics Office of Mongolia, *Mongolian Statistical Yearbook, 1998* (Ulaanbaatar, 1999),18.

7. *World Almanac and Book of Facts 2000* (Mahwah, NJ: World Almanac Books, 1999), 841.

8. Academy of Sciences MPR, *Information Mongolia*, 56.

9. National Statistics Office of Mongolia, *Mongolian Statistical Yearbook 1999*, 28.

10. Ibid., 51.

11. *World Almanac 2000*, 841.

12. Academy of Sciences MPR, *Information Mongolia*, 87. New research suggests that this date is still controversial.

13. David Morgan, *The Mongols* (Cambridge, MA: Blackwell, 1990), 44-49, 281; Paul Kahn, *The Secret History of the Mongols: The Origin of Chingis Khan* (Boston: Cheng and Tsui, 1998), xvi-xvii.

14. Bat-erdene Batbayar (Baabar), *Twentieth Century Mongolia*, by Christopher Kaplonski (Cambridge: Cambridge University Press, 1999), 23.

15. Paul Ratchnevsky, *Genghis Khan: His Life and Legacy* (Oxford: Blackwell, 1991).

16. Batbayar, *Twentieth Century Mongolia*, 27; Morgan, *The Mongols*, 61-174; Ratchnevsky, *Genghis Khan*, 169-174.

17. Academy of Sciences MPR, *Information Mongolia*, 104-105.

18. Morgan, *The Mongols*, 199-204; Academy of Sciences MPR, *Information Mongolia*, 103.

19. Ibid., 111-112.

Chapter 2

The Twentieth Century

From Domination to Democracy

NASAN DASHDENDEVIIN BUMAA

THE STORY OF OUR PEOPLE is one of incessant struggle for national independence and personal freedom, the key factors for creating a good and fulfilling life for our children and us. Our history is always tempered by our harsh climate and difficult location, for we have been buffeted by Siberian winds no more than by our two giant neighbors, Russia and China. Their internal affairs and foreign policies have directly influenced our history.

At the End of Manchu Rule: 1900-1911

Despite the Manchu (Qing) Dynasty's 200-year oppressive rule of Mongolia, my people still retained our language, culture, and native traditions. According to the 1918 census, the population of Mongolia had just reached 648,000, one-fifth of whom were Chinese and Russian. As the land was so vast and the population so sparse, fewer than one person occupied a square kilometer. In comparison, the United States had 15.3 people per square kilometer then.

The majority of Mongolians were herders, tending over 12 million horses, cows, yaks, camels, sheep, and goats, all referred to as cattle. They lived in collapsible *ger*s, as it was not unusual for them to move eight to ten times a year.[1] My great-grandfather Nasan, a nomad, moved frequently with his cattle. Even Ih Huree (or Ikh Khuree, later named Ulaanbaatar) moved over twenty times between its

founding in 1639 and 1855, the year the city settled in its present location.[2]

Mongolian nomadic life was adapted to the land and the Continental climate, which dictated the use of specific methods of cattle raising. As a result, the Mongolian language is extremely rich in pastoral terminology. There are over 160 ways to count the age of livestock, over 300 ways to distinguish their color, over 400 terms for their organs, and another 100 descriptive terms for animal behavior. There are more than 30 ways to name a horse's stride.[3]

Mongolia was not totally isolated; countries other than China and Russia began trading (usually fur trading) and developing gold and coal mines in the early twentieth century. In fact, there were so many foreigners that they formed separate districts in Ih Huree.

By the end of Manchu rule, the Mongolian people were divided into a strict hierarchy of social classes more complicated than the European feudal system of the Middle Ages. At the top of the hierarchy were the Manchu emperor and his administrators in Mongolia and China. The upper echelon of the Mongolian class system consisted of the descendants of Genghis Khan, the princes (*noyod*) and noblemen (*taij nar*). While many were very wealthy, natural disasters or personal calamities had caused some to lose their herds and their wealth. However, even if they were poor, they did not lose their noble title.

Serfs served various masters. The first group of serfs (nomads, really), the *albat ard*, owed

Map 5.
Mongolia under
Manchu Dynasty rule
(ca. 1900).

Figure 2.1.
Women in traditional
headdress with dung
baskets collecting
dung for the fire,
Bayanhongor Aimag.
(NMMH, 1920s)

Figure 2.2.
Prince Namsrai with his
wife, Ih Huree.
(NMMH, 1910)

Figure 2.3. Khutuktu Tsedenbaljir of Sain Noyon Khan Aimag, a high reincarnated lama. (NMMH, 1921)

Figure 2.4, below. The students of a Buddhist (lama) school in Ih Huree. (NMMH, pre-1920)

paid taxes to their overlords in the form of taxes and services to the Manchu: military duty (including annual training camp and border guard service), upkeep and service for the horse-relay system (the administrative highway–the equivalent of the American Pony Express), cultivation of state land, and herding state cattle. The *ard albat* also owed taxes and services to the *noyod* and *taij nar* of their district.

A second group of serfs, the *hamjilga*, was attached to the *noyod* and *taij nar*. These serfs paid taxes to their overlords in the form of livestock and performed duties (corvée labor) in their overlords' household. Their owners could decide their fate as they pleased, transferring them to other lords or marrying them to anyone they wished.

There were also commoners, herders, and administrators. While they did not owe fealty to the Manchu administration or Mongolian overlords, they did pay taxes. Again, they could range from very rich to poor.

In addition to the secular hierarchy described above, there was a religious hierarchy of Buddhist lamas, headed by the Bogd Gegeen in Ih Huree. While some lamas were very wealthy, others remained miserably poor. Of the small Mongolian population (see above), more than 100,000 men (almost half the adult male population) were lamas, one-third of them residing in about 700 temples across the country.

The wealthy lamas, like the princes and noblemen, maintained their own group of serfs, named *shav*, who paid taxes to and performed duties for the lama lords. These serfs were exempt from Manchu administrative duties and taxes.

By the twentieth century, the Buddhist religion had deeply penetrated Mongolian culture, and people lived and prayed according to the teachings of their lama. Shamanism, the traditional Mongolian religion, was practiced only in the peripheral areas of the country .[4] The only schools were Buddhist, and they taught exclusively Tibetan religious material in the Tibetan script. The Mongolian script was largely forgotten.

These social and religious structures made life harsh for many. The economic structure also punished the Mongolians. As there were few markets in the country, Chinese and other merchants acted as middlemen between Mongolians and foreign markets. The merchants bought Mongolian goods (mostly animals and their by-products) and sold imported items back to them. The merchants tried to buy Mongolian goods at the lowest price and sell them imported goods at the highest price. This left the Mongolians no choice but to buy on credit, which resulted in most owing such high debts to the merchants that they were never able to repay them.

The commoners and serfs intermittently protested Manchu rule. Some organized riots and secret resistance groups; others fled from their overlords to other aimags where they could start anew. There were also courageous Robin Hoods who robbed cattle from the rich and distributed them to the poor. Those who were caught had to face the cruel step-by-step methods of torture practiced by the Manchu government.

The Fight for Independence and Freedom: 1911-1921

The Manchu Dynasty had long maintained a policy of preventing Chinese settlement in

Figure 2.5. A Mongolian being tortured during Manchu Dynasty rule. (NMMH, ca. 1910)

*Figure 2.6.
Portrait of the
Bogd Khan by the
artist Balduugin
Sharav (1869-
1939). (Fine Arts
Museum,
Ulaanbaatar, early
twentieth century)*

Mongolia. Only itinerant Chinese merchants without their families were allowed to work in Mongolia. However, in the early twentieth century the Empress Dowager Tzu-Hsi (Cixi) implemented a "New Government Policy," mandating the Chinese settlement of Mongolia. Her purpose was to encourage agriculture and assimilate the Mongolians into Chinese society through intermarriage. The ultimate purpose of the policy was to reduce Mongo-

lia's status to a Chinese province, like Inner Mongolia.

Since the New Government Policy threatened the very existence of Mongolia, people from all levels of society united in opposition to it. Even the lamas, who preached humility, engaged in fistfights with the Chinese and looted their companies.[5]

The Buddhist religious leader of Mongolia, the Bogd Javzandamba VIII (the Bogd

Gegeen[6]), along with the high princes and lamas seized this historical opportunity to seek national independence. In 1900, they sent official delegates to Russia in order to gain support for a Mongolian independence movement. When the Tibetan Dalai Lama visited Ih Huree in 1904, the Mongolian leaders sought his support as well.[7]

In 1911 the high princes and lamas gathered in Ih Huree and decided to proclaim an independent Mongolian nation. They sent Prince Handdorj (Khanddorj) to Russia to request aid. Russia promised to take measures to reverse the New Government Policy and sent soldiers to Ih Huree to protect the Russian consulate.

The Chinese people also began to object to Manchurian rule, beginning with their reaction to the Boxer Rebellion (spring 1900) and ending with the Wuchang Revolt (October 1911), which sparked the actual 1911 revolution. Using this opportunity, the Bogd Javzandamba VIII proclaimed that the time was right for Mongolia to separate from the Manchu. His decree of independence, announced on December 1, 1911, became the call for a united struggle.[8] On December 29, the Bogd Javzandamba VIII was proclaimed the Bogd Khan, the religious and state leader of Mongolia.[9] Thus began the tumultuous era of Mongolia's struggle for independence.

The commoners began confiscating Chinese property and burning their houses; the Chinese merchants fled in fear. The revolution extended beyond Ih Huree to the western aimags. When the first fifty Mongolian soldiers marched from the capital to free Hovd, the major western administrative unit, new recruits joined them until the revolutionary army reached 5,000. This large force easily freed Hovd from foreign forces.[10]

In neighboring China, the 1911 revolution resulted in the founding of a presidential Republic on January 1, 1912. The new rulers still considered Mongolia a Chinese province even though Mongolia wanted to be independent. China's great size and strategic position left Mongolia quite vulnerable, so its leaders sought support from Russia. The Mongolian government tried to initiate negotiations between Russia and China to have them recognize Mongolia as an independent nation, but it

did not succeed. It then sent representatives to Japan and appealed for help to England, France, and the United States, but the American leaders felt that Mongolia belonged to China,[11] and the great nations became too busy during World War I to devote their attention to far-off Mongolia.

In 1915, China, Russia, and Mongolia signed a treaty that granted Mongolia autonomy but under the suzerainty of China. Mongolia's authority was limited to the right to decide economic matters regarding domestic industry and foreign trade. Inner Mongolia officially became part of the newly established Chinese republic.

Around this time, Mongolia instituted some progressive changes. The Bogd Khan became the official head of government; the leadership established an Upper Parliament, consisting of the Prime Minister and his ministers, and a Lower Parliament of government secretaries and military representatives. These assemblies had the right and responsibility to advise the Bogd Khan. Russia provided military and financial aid as well as the means to establish secular schools, newspapers, electricity and telecommunication centers, European-style veterinary services, and shops. However, the Chinese merchants continued to dominate trade between Mongolia and the outside world.[12]

In 1919, civil wars broke out in Russia and China. Still, they did not forget Mongolia for a moment. The Chinese general Shui Shu-Chien destroyed Mongolian autonomy in January 1920. During the ceremony of dissolution, the Bogd Khan was made to bow before a picture of the Chinese president, which caused great anger among Mongolians.

There was nothing for Mongolia to do but ask for aid from abroad. As the Bolsheviks were busy fighting the White (Czarist) Russians–sometimes on Mongolian soil—Mongolia again appealed to the United States and Japan, but neither sent aid.[13]

Learning that they had to rely on themselves, many Mongolians formed armed resistance groups against the Chinese in 1920.[14] One such group was the Mongolian People's Party (MPP). With the support of some noblemen and the Bogd Khan, this new organization sent representatives to Russia to meet

Figure 2.7. Suhbaatar with Amgayev, his Buriad Russian Comintern mentor for communism and military strategy. (NMMH, 1922)

with the Soviet Comintern, the Communist Party's political organization that had the responsibility to spread communism to other nations. Suhbaatar carried a petition with the Bogd Khan's stamp hidden inside his riding crop. At the meeting, the young Mongolian revolutionaries requested Bolshevik support for their fight for independence. The Bolshevik leaders urged the Mongolian revolutionaries to write a new letter in their own name, rather than in the Bogd Khan's name. Once they did so, the Bolsheviks provided aid, and with it, ideological influence. [15]

With Bolshevik help, the Mongolian revolutionaries organized the government and armed forces, appointing S. Danzan as Party leader and D. Suhbaatar as head of the mili-

tary. The new government's goals were to (a) unite all internal resistance forces to free the homeland from foreign occupation, (b) establish a democratic government, and (c) unite all Mongolian nationalities into one independent nation.[16]

A joint Mongolian-Bolshevik army entered the capital and routed the foreign military from central Mongolia in July 1921. The revolutionaries established a limited monarchy under the Bogd Khan and named Bodoo the Prime Minister.

Military actions in other parts of the country finally ended foreign occupation. My grandfather Nanzad and his younger brother Purev were revolutionaries who fought in Hovd and Uliastai.

Independence and Communism: 1922-1928

The new government was faced with two questions: how to reorganize the country's political, economic, and social structures and how to gain international recognition. As Genghis Khan had instructed, "It is easy to conquer the whole world on a horse, but it is not easy to get off the horse and manage the state."

The revolutionary leaders invited representatives from all levels of society to help form a People's Government and replace the old feudal society with a new social structure. This government abolished the ranks and titles of the princes and noblemen and rescinded their right to own serfs. Serfs became free citizens. The People's Government laid the foundation for secular elementary school education, science centers, and museums.

The Mongolian economy boomed in the early transition years, the number of Chinese merchants rising from 863 to 1462, American and German traders from 5 to 62, and Mongolian traders from 234 to 635.[1]

The new Soviet Comintern gradually imposed its Communist ideology on the Mongolian leadership and, through them, the entire population. Russian revolutionary leader Lenin met Mongolian representatives in November 1921 and advised them "to leap over the capitalist stage [of cultural evolution], going directly from feudalism to communism."[18] Mongolian People's Party members who disagreed with this policy were persecuted or assassinated. First Prime Minister Bodoo, who tried to establish diplomatic relations with the United States, was beheaded. Next D. Suhbaatar, hero of the revolution, met an mysterious death after he suggested that the Russian army should quit Mongolian soil.[19]

Figure 2.8. A recreation of Lenin greeting the Mongolian delegation, led by S. Danzan, in November 1921. (From a painting by A. Setsentokhio, in The Contemporary Art of Mongolia, *1971)*

Figure 2.9. Danzan with his Harley-Davidson, Ih Huree. (NMMH, 1922)

Then Danzan was executed after he recommended that Mongolia become capitalist. At the time of his death (June 1924), Danzan was the local representative of an Anglo-American automobile company. He had three private houses, several cars, and a Harley-Davidson.[20]

In May 1924 the Bogd Khan died. A month later the Mongolian People's Party (MPP) decided to reorganize the government along the lines of a republic. In November they held the First National Assembly, which approved a new constitution. This constitution declared Mongolia to be a republic and granted democratic rights and freedoms to all citizens except those labeled class exploiters.

During the November National Assembly, the MPP made visible Mongolia's connection to communism and Soviet Russia. The Party changed its name from the Mongolian People's Party to the Mongolian People's Revolutionary Party (MPRP), a clear symbol of Communist orientation. And the National Assem-

bly delegates renamed the capital city Ulaanbaatar, meaning Red Hero, a Sovietized term.

Even though the Party's name was officially changed to MPRP, the Party still had not become totally committed to communism. Prime Minister Tserendorj, the Party's leader, along with the nation's statesmen and intelligentsia, preferred a more democratic structure than the one recommended by the Soviet Comintern. The national leaders also desired to expand diplomatic and trade relations with other nations and prevent Russia from meddling in domestic affairs. To this end, the government sent Mongolian children to schools in Germany and France as well as Russia.

In 1926, the key motto was "Get Rich," which reflected the national desire to develop private property and a capitalist economy. The government encouraged foreign investment, and merchants and businessmen from Germany, America, and Denmark expanded their activities in Mongolia. German advisors helped build the brick industry and the first small electrical station. This was not what Lenin had envisioned for Mongolia.

About that time, the Soviet Union's Communist Party was facing its own internal strife, and criticism of the extreme Bolshevik view in Russia created favorable conditions for independent Mongolian development for a little while. However, the Soviet Comintern soon demanded obeisance from the MPRP's Central Committee, threatening the withdrawal of Soviet aid if Mongolia did not comply.[21]

When Stalin became Secretary General of the Soviet Union's Communist Party in the late 1920s, he established a dictatorship. The Soviet Comintern representatives in Mongolia then led a coup d'état, removing the rightist Mongolians (who were in favor of some capitalist development) from Party membership in 1928. This marked the end of Mongolian self-determination along capitalist lines and the beginning of the imposition of Communist ideology on the Mongolian population.

Settling in to Communism: 1928 Through the 1930s

Efforts to impose socialism (i.e., the government owns the nation's resources and controls

Figure 2.10. Poster urging the common people to expel lamas, capitalists, etc., from their midst: "We must clean out the enemies of the people from the cooperatives." (NMMH, 1928-1932)

their use; everyone works for the government and draws a salary from the State) on all aspects of Mongolian life increased, starting in 1928. With pressure and support from the Soviet Union, the Mongolian Communist Party leadership undertook multiple reforms. Under the pretense of establishing a government of the common people, the leadership removed the old nobility, the wealthy class, and pre-revolutionary government officials from political office. Labeled enemies of the people, their property was confiscated and many were sent to prison. The government levied heavy taxes on the Buddhist temples, seized their property, and forced the lamas and their clerks to become civilians. Revolutionary young men and women who had cut their long hair and wore Russian-style caps to separate themselves from the old traditions helped the government. In order to delete everything that was considered backwards and archaic from the new society, these young people stormed into people's houses, destroying their gods and sacred objects.

The government also confiscated common people's property and began to force the nomadic herders into co-operatives, where their cattle became public property. When in 1929 the State acquired the exclusive right to engage in international trade and limited it to Soviet trade, private business practically ended. Thus Mongolians became isolated from the rest of the world just as an economic crisis (exacerbated by the world-wide Great Depression) caused severe shortages in food and material products.

Many Mongolians resisted the Soviet Union and Mongolian Communist Party's policies. Over 30,000 people from the western and southern aimags emigrated to China in the 1930s.[22] When Mongolian troops tried to retrieve them, the nobility, lamas, and thousands of commoners rose in armed resistance to the Communist regime, spreading through six aimags in 1931-32. The protesters, equipped with guns, wooden sticks, knives, and anything they could grab, were quickly subdued by a modern army of cannon, tanks, and planes.

During these years of unrest when thousands of people were murdered, the Mongolian economy rapidly declined, and the herds suffered immense losses partly due to inclement weather. It is estimated that between 1930 and 1932, the herds were reduced from 23.6 million to 16.1 million, a terrible loss.[23]

Accepting that the policy of rapid conversion to socialism was not working, the government made some attempt to reduce unrest in the countryside. It supported innovations aimed at stimulating economic growth, even ones that were not socialist. In 1933-1934, the agricultural industry and wool treatment factories of Hatgal (Khatgal) were established, and for the first time Mongolia began process-

Figure 2.11. Mongolian revolutionary youth confiscate the property of the wealthy class. (NMMH, 1929)

Figure 2.12.
This painting is a
re-creation of a
1930s poster.
Whereas the
original
emphasized the
glory of the
People's Army
destroying the
wealthy lamas and
princes, this 1990s
poster sympathizes
with the victims of
the Purges.
(Museum of the
Purges)

Figure 2.13. Poster urging people to learn to write in the Latin alphabet to honor the tenth anniversary of the Revolution. The slogan at the top is the Mongolian version of Marx's phrase, "Workers of the world, unite!" (NMMH, 1931)

Figure 2.14. The author's parents when they moved from Hentii Aimag to Ulaanbaatar. (Nasan Dashdendeviin Bumaa, ca. 1950)

ing its raw agricultural products.

Literature, theatre, and cinematography reflecting national and revolutionary themes developed at this time. The State initiated mass literacy campaigns, trying unsuccessfully to first teach the ancient Mongolian script and then replace it with Latin letters. Even though the state established free primary and secondary schools, teachers had to urge or even force the herders to send their children regularly. Parents still wanted their children helping with the herds or preferred to have their sons trained as lamas. My father learned the traditional Mongolian script from an acquaintance and began attending a temple school in 1932. One year later he entered the local elementary school. After he graduated, he began teaching there. My mother was not so lucky. Although she loved school, her mother pulled her out of middle school because she was needed at home. Only her older sister was allowed to advance through middle school.

Purges and War: Late 1930s through World War II

Just as Mongolia had been caught in the internal problems of its neighbors in the revolutionary period, so it became embroiled in international politics in the 1930s. In 1931 Japan invaded Manchuria, Barga, and Inner Mongolia; in 1935, it began a military campaign against Mongolia. The Soviet Union leadership and its representatives in Mongolia declared that "enemies of the Revolution" and "Japanese spies" were living in Mongolia and needed to be cleansed from the general population. Owen Lattimore compared this situation to the paranoia of the "Red danger" that spread throughout the United States after World War II.[24] In 1933, the Mongolian government created a new category, "Japanese spies against the Revolution," and severely punished 317 people, sent 126 to the Russian *gulag*,

Figure 2.15. This poster tells the people of Inner Mongolia and Barga that every time they make an offering to the Bogd Banchin, a Tibetan lama, he and the Inner Mongolian feudal princes give it to Japan. Japan will then use the money to invade Mongolia, which is the cousin of Inner Mongolia. (NMMH, early 1930s)

Figure 2.16. General Secretary Choibalsan (on the right) in a Marshal's uniform when he was Prime Minister, Minister of Foreign Affairs, Minister of the Army, and Commander-in-chief. With him is his eventual successor, Tsedenbal who was then Vice Minister and Commander of the Department of Politics (responsible for Communist ideology), Ulaanbaatar. (NMMH, 1944)

and repatriated 400 Russian Buriad families (which had relocated in eastern Mongolia following the Russian revolution). The aim of this policy was to create divisions and animosity between the ethnic groups of Mongolia.[25]

Against the background of international instability, the Mongolian Communist Party began cracking down on all opposition. They destroyed those who sought to preserve Mongolian traditions, closing the temples and killing the Buddhist lamas with brutal force. Blaming the 1932 popular uprising on the lamas, Stalin demanded that they be exterminated or else he would withdraw aid from Mongolia. The Mongolian prime ministers, Genden and Amar, refused to comply with Stalin's demands. They were brought to the Soviet Union where they were assassinated.

In 1936, emulating the Soviet Union's KGB (secret police force), Mongolia established its own Ministry of the Interior, which was responsible for oppression and the purges. Choibalsan, who had been one of the major partisans in the 1921 revolution and Vice Minister under Genden, became its Minister and oversaw the purges. In 1936 he was proclaimed Minister of the Army, and in 1939 he stepped from that position into Prime Minis-

ter. In his first year as Prime Minister, the rest of the Party leaders were purged from the Communist Party's Central Committee, and Choibalsan became dictator until his death in 1952.[26]

In August 1937 the Soviet Union's Vice Minister of the Interior, Frinovskii, visited Mongolia where he revealed the supposed "Japanese plan of the invasion of Mongolia." He gave the MPRP leadership a list of names of 115 Mongolian inhabitants who were considered Japanese accomplices and recommended that these people be "purged," that is, demoted, punished, or killed. Thus he started the second wave of purges that quickly swept over the country. Starting on September 10, 1937, many thousands of people from the Communist Party, the central and provincial governments, lamas, and commoners were named "enemy of the Revolution," "the people's enemy," or "Japanese spy" and purged. The intelligentsia—writers, poets, and scientists—were also arrested and their work was burned. Between 1933 and 1953, the incomplete official records reveal that more than 36,000 people were victims of the Purges.[27] In fact, we still do not have a complete account of the number of people who were killed. All we know is that every household and every level of society experienced these senseless purges.

The main purpose of such ruthless measures was obviously to eliminate potential opposition to Communist control of the government. The Purges may also have been used to stop the unification of ethnic groups, assure Mongolia's dependence on the Soviet Union, and destroy the nomadic culture. The Purges basically destroyed an entire generation of Mongolians[28] and laid the foundation for political oppression, dictatorship, the hegemony of Communist ideology, neglect of the Mongolian tradition, and the destruction of freedom of speech.

This internal war was soon replaced by a real war threat. In 1939 Japan entered Mongolian territory again, starting an undeclared war. The united Mongolian and Soviet forces fought against the Japanese in the summer of 1939 and soon chased them out of Mongolia. When the Japanese military returned at the

Figure 2.17. Published in Moscow, this poster commemorates the defeat of the Japanese army through Mongolian-Soviet cooperation in World War II. (NMMH, 1945)

end of World War II (in 1945), the joint Mongolian-Soviet forces defeated them once more.

During World War II, under the motto "All for the front, all for victory," Mongolia supported the USSR's war effort by providing much-needed supplies and military troops. To further help the war effort, Mongolia doubled its exports to the Soviet Union, depleting the herds (by an estimated 6 million, partly the result of drought and a calamitous winter) and living with fewer Soviet imports, as the meat and supplies were needed to support Soviet troops. Mongolia suffered a reduced standard of living, as did the USSR. Still, some good things came out of the war: development of the food industry, increase in domestic trade, introduction of primary schools at the local level in rural areas, an increased number of secondary schools, and the establishment of the first university, Mongolia State University in Ulaanbaatar.[29]

At the February 1945 Yalta Conference, Roosevelt, Churchill, and Stalin discussed the question of Mongolian independence. The great leaders decided to preserve the status quo, which boosted Mongolian independence in the international realm. On October 20, 1945, Mongolia held a referendum, and the people voted unanimously for independence. Soon after, China officially recognized Mongolia's independence.

Leaping Over Capitalism to Socialism: Post-World War II to 1959

After World War II, several European and Asian countries including China formed Communist governments, and many Mongolians believed that socialism would win the Cold War. In Mongolia, Choibalsan's cult of personality reached fanatic proportions while Stalin's writings were memorized as though they were holy script and some children were named Marx, Engels, Lenin, and Stalin.

Figure 2.18. Vista of Ulaanbaatar from the State Department Store. The round building straight ahead is the famous Mongolian Circus; the other buildings are apartments. (NMMH, 1981)

This international brotherhood of socialist countries supported Mongolia's economic development. Chairman Mao Zedong of China established positive relations between China and Mongolia, paving the way for Chinese aid. The rail line that had previously linked the USSR with Ulaanbaatar now reached all the way to Beijing. Chinese workers were sent to Ulaanbaatar to help build official and administrative buildings as well as housing units for civilians.

Beginning in the 1950s, the USSR and China, now both Communist governments, started competing with each other by giving numerous aid packages and loans to Mongolia.[30] By the end of the decade, other Communist countries such as Czechoslovakia, East Germany, Bulgaria, and Hungary provided technical and professional help for the development of factories (shoe, leather, flour and other processed food, textiles, knitted garments, wooden items, and housing material factories). In 1959, 76 percent of Mongolian net exports went to the USSR, 15.25 percent to Eastern Europe, and 4 percent to China.[31]

Ulaanbaatar became unrecognizable with its new factories, offices, housing complexes, asphalt roads, central heating system, sanitation, and modern water supply. The city that used to consist of temples, felt *ger*s, and wood-fenced properties received a face-lift as a result of international support.[32]

The Mongolian people were full of enthusiasm for this new society. They willingly changed to the Cyrillic (Russian) alphabet and worked at increasing literacy. Primary school education became compulsory, and secondary education was phased in all over the country during the 1960s. Theater, music, cinematography, the famous Mongolian Circus, museums, and libraries grew. The new themes in art were industrialization, urbanization, and railroad building. The new literature portrayed common workers as heroes, while merchants and the wealthy were portrayed with antipathy. By creating these new hero-images, the arts influenced people's minds.

Big efforts were made to connect rural areas

with medical centers and emergency services, and special medical expeditions brought medicine and prophylactic measures into the countryside to block the spread of contagious diseases.[33]

At the same time that Mongolians were experiencing so much progress in national development, underlying problems would occasionally burst forth. The State enforced strict obeisance to Marxist-Leninist teachings accompanied by the discouragement of Mongolian culture, tradition, and nationalism. In 1949, the newly created Media and Literature Censorship Office mandated certain restrictions on the teaching of Mongolian history and literature, including any positive interpretation of Genghis Khan's military campaigns or politico-social order.

Two of the groups that paid a high price for the transition to communism were the intelligentsia and the herders. The intelligentsia, whose members had begun the postwar period full of enthusiasm and optimism that their insight–and critique of government policies–could help build a great society, ended the 1950s stripped of their official posi-

Figure 2.19. Herders and their children learning to read Cyrillic. (NMMH, late 1940s)

tions, exiled from their urban homes, and bereft of their human rights and personal freedoms.[34]

The herders, who were facing new restrictions, experienced displacement as well. Although the collectivization policy had been in effect since the early days of communism, the postwar period saw its enforcement. In 1949, the government required every herder to raise the number of cattle by 50 percent per year, regardless of disasters, natural or otherwise. They were also expected to produce set amounts of meat, wool, and milk required by the State's five-year plans.[35] In 1954, the government decreed that all livestock must be put into state-owned cooperatives, as was appropriate for a non-capitalist nation. By 1959, all herders had been forced into collectives where they followed the State's five-year plans. The government permitted herders to keep a small number of private livestock along with the State herds.

It is not surprising that many sought to find work that was less risky and onerous and

Figure 2.20. Mongolia is depicted in this poster as leaping over capitalism, moving directly from feudalism to socialism with the help of the Soviets. The artist D. Amgalan paints capitalism as a black stripe, a dark time, while communism is in red, a bright positive time. (NMMH, 1984)

more rewarding than herding and agriculture. And so multitudes left the countryside and moved to the cities where they were welcomed into the growing labor force needed by the new industries.

Efforts to socialize property continued in the cities as well. The State seized all trade cooperatives, forcing people involved in private trading, handcraft, and service sectors to participate in State-owned cooperatives. As if this move was not enough transition for workers, the State soon replaced its own cooperatives with State-owned factories.

By the end of the 1950s, the State had realized its goal of destroying private property and transforming Mongolia from feudalism to socialism. It had accomplished Lenin's goal of having Mongolia leap over capitalism on its path toward socialism and communism. But the cost to the general population was high. Tsedenbal, who had become dictator following Choibalsan's death in 1952, helped increase the exclusive privileges, powers and rights of the MPRP leadership. The Party's control over the population grew even stronger.[36]

Communist Mongolia: 1960–1989

In the 1960s, the Communist Party strengthened Mongolia's international position, becoming a member of the United Nations in 1961 and the Council for Economic Mutual Assistance (COMECON, the umbrella organization of Soviet-bloc countries that coordinated economic development and trade) in 1962. Soon Great Britain, Finland, France, and other Western nations officially recognized Mongolia (although the United States did not establish diplomatic relations until 1987).

However, in 1966-69, Chairman Mao Zedong initiated the Cultural Revolution in China, which caused deteriorating relations between China and the USSR. As Mongolia was under Russian protection, it had to pull back from its good relations with China. The Chinese workers who had been helping to build Mongolia's infrastructure left, and the Russian soldiers came. Along the Sino-Mongolian border, Russian and Mongolian military divisions stood face-to-face with the Chinese border patrol on the other side. When China tested its hydro-missile system in June 1967, the Soviets created an anti-missile protection system around Ulaanbaatar similar to the one around Moscow.[37]

Figure 2.21. A sewing factory, one of the main industries in Communist times. (NMMH, 1981)

*Figure 2.22.
The author's father-in-law as a young man making notes about the woman's milk products (clotted cream and leftovers) for the government. (Nasan Dashdendeviin Bumaa, 1960s)*

Trade between the two countries increased, and the Soviet support that had taken hold in the 1950s accelerated in the1960s. Industrial growth is reflected in the labor statistics for this era. In 1963, 46.5 percent of the total population consisted of factory and office workers; by 1985 this percentage increased to 65.1 percent. Concomitantly, the percentage of herders and artisans decreased from 53.3 in 1963 to 34.9 in 1985.[38]

Industrial growth was matched by population growth. Mongolia achieved its highest birth rate between 1969 and 1979.[39] Encouraged by the State, my parents-in-law had twelve children! That is how Mongolia reached 2 million in 1988.[40]

In the countryside, herders were expected to live in specialized farm divisions. To entice them to settle on these farm factories, the herding cooperatives and farm centers built modern barns and wells; they became service and cultural centers for light industry, food pro-

cessing, and electricity production. Herders remained nomadic, but they were integrated into the socialist economy because they raised herds for the State and received a salary in exchange. My mother-in-law worked on a farm that specialized in milk products. She recalls that she had to wake up very early to milk many cows so that her cooperative could meet its government-imposed quota and she could receive her salary.

Herders also "modernized" by replacing about 90 percent of their *ger* furnishings with factory-made items.[41] They took to the socialist lifestyle up to a point, for they would not eat vegetables, leaving them to rot when they moved camp.

Life became a little better for all Mongolians. National flour-processing factories produced bread, cookies, biscuits, pasta, and sweets for national consumption. National TV started broadcasting in 1967, and soon city families could watch TV in their homes. In the 1970s,

82.4 percent of the total Mongolian population had become educated, and UNESCO awarded Mongolia international recognition for educational achievement.[42] Mongolians started contributing to national and international science. In 1981, the Mongolian cosmonaut J. Gurragchaa flew in space as a member of the Soviet team. And Mongolian athletes participated in international competitions, winning numerous medals in the Olympics and other world championships. Meanwhile, back home, Mongolians enjoyed performing and watching the world's classical music, opera, theatre, and ballet.

Mongolia also had more opportunity to learn about the West. The national and Soviet TV channels broadcast a limited number of Western shows, even though they were heavily censored. Several thousand Mongolian students studying in Eastern European countries had glimpses of the West, for there the Iron Curtain was not so controlled as it was in Mongolia. Still, students in the cities began emulating Western styles, especially the Beatles' long hair and bell-bottom trousers. While the school authorities admonished these rash youth, there was no punishment as there would have been in the past.

Many Mongolians became interested in Western literature that had been translated into Mongolian. I was totally absorbed in Mark Twain's *Tom Sawyer* and *The Adventures of Huckleberry Finn*. This freedom was balanced by newspaper stories condemning American imperialism and predicting Mongolia's bright future under communism. To me, these predictions seemed far away.

Mongolians' glimpse of Western life was only a taste. In reality, freedom of expression had ceased to exist and human rights were severely limited. The renowned Mongolian poet R. Choinom, while serving a political sentence in prison in 1970 for criticizing socialism, wrote:

We tried to renounce God, and worshiped a one-man rule instead;

We smelled the blood from the confusions and mistakes we have made.

When rushing to develop [our country], we turned in the wrong directions,

But we patched all our mistakes and established socialist rule![43]

Incredible as it might seem, even a central member of the Politburo was not exempt from punishment for failing to toe the Party line. In 1962, D. Tumor-Ochir was responsible for organizing the 800-year anniversary of Genghis Khan's birth. Tumor-Ochir planned to raise a statue in Genghis Khan's birthplace and create postage stamps in commemoration of this great event. However, the Russians were afraid that a big celebration would spark nationalistic sentiments when the Communist goal was to build loyalty to an international workforce. So the Mongolian authorities arrested Tumor-Ochir and exiled him to a distant aimag.

By the end of the 1980s, the Communist Party and administrative personnel had become a huge state bureaucracy whose inner circle carefully selected all representatives to local government and remained in their own positions for twenty-five to thirty years. Their children became part of the elite echelon in a supposedly classless society. Mongolia was totally dependent on the Soviet Union, mainly Russia, which did not promote economic independence and freedom. Nor did it develop the expertise or infrastructure necessary to bring sustainable economic development for such a large territory. No one was responsible for property, and the monstrous industries were run with outdated, inefficient technology that destroyed the surrounding environment and wasted natural resources. And while government costs increased annually, personal income levels decreased. Thus the conflict between the negative and positive aspects of socialism continued.

Democratic Mongolia: 1989 to the Present

By 1989, the Mongolian people were well aware of the problems in their government, which had initiated the same basic reforms that General Secretary Gorbachev had in the Soviet Union. But we were not prepared for the total collapse of communism in one country after another. First Poland, then other Eastern bloc nations and even Russia declared in 1991 that national-level communism is not viable. In November 1989 the Berlin Wall was

torn down as East Germany joined West Germany. This act spurred Mongolians to oppose the Communist government.

In Ulaanbaatar, young Mongolians quickly formed an activist group and began posting political slogans and news on the streets. Within a month, they formed the Mongolian Democratic Union (MDU), naming S. Zorig, a young lecturer in scientific communism at Mongolian State University, their leader and spokesman. They scheduled their first demonstration against the Communist government for December 10, 1989, International Human Rights Day. On that day, they started the demonstration with the song, "The Sound of the Bell":

The darkness choked the words I wanted to say;
It clouded the eyes with which I wanted to see.
But luckily, the bell rang!
With great effort, I woke from the nightmare.
Let the bell's sound wake us up!
The sound of the bell is waking us![44]

Just as Americans rang the bell of freedom when proclaiming their independence two centuries ago, so the bell of independence and freedom rang in the minds of Mongolians as they joined the peaceful demonstration on that cold December day. The demonstrators sang, holding hands and calling for people to join the fight against communism. They held signs that read, "We need a multi-party system," or "Let us respect human rights to the fullest."[45]

Peaceful demonstrations quickly spread across the country. Thousands of people were involved, filling to capacity the major squares and plazas of Mongolia. Our people demanded the abolition of one-party oppression, *glasnost'* and *perestroika*; respect for human rights, equality, justice, and pluralism; freedom of the media; and transition from the centrally planned economy of communism to the market economy of capitalism.

On March 7, 1990, the democratic forces in Ulaanbaatar held a hunger strike in Suhbaatar Square, the main square facing the parliament

building. Their stated purpose was to force the resignation of the MPRP Central Committee and establish a Provisionary People's Assembly that would restructure government along democratic and capitalist lines. Despite the winter cold, many people gathered in the square and remained there until nightfall, discussing the events or supporting the hunger strikers. Some looked bewildered, others amused or concerned.

Representatives of the MPRP leadership met with representatives from the new MDU to discuss the situation. Both sides made concessions. At the conclusion of the meeting, the delegates announced to the people that the Communist government would meet the demands of the hunger strikers. The hunger strike ended before any of the participants became ill or died.

The hunger strike served as a shock that triggered popular involvement in the democratic social movement. As increasing numbers of people decided to join the movement, they formed new political parties, including the Mongolian Democratic Party (MDP), the Mongolian Social Democratic Party (MSDP), the Mongolian National Democratic Party

(MNDP), the Freedom Labor Party (FLP), and the Mongolian Green Party (MGP). My colleagues at the Institute of History at the Academy of Sciences became members of these new parties; I joined the FLP, which supported private business in the hope of stimulating rapid economic development.

In spring 1990, it seemed as if all Mongolians were involved in politics. People avidly read the new political parties' newspapers as they prepared for the first democratic, multiparty election in almost seventy years. In the July election, the MPRP received 60 percent of the total votes, while the new political parties received 40 percent. Even though the MPRP won the majority of seats in Parliament, the new Prime Minister D. Byambasuren appointed two opposition leaders (D. Ganbold of the MNDP and Dorligjav of the MDP) to his cabinet.

The new government quickly got down to business, working on a new constitution that would restructure the more permanent government to follow. After over a year of committee work and debate among all representatives, this "Little Parliament" ratified the new Mongolian National Constitution on January

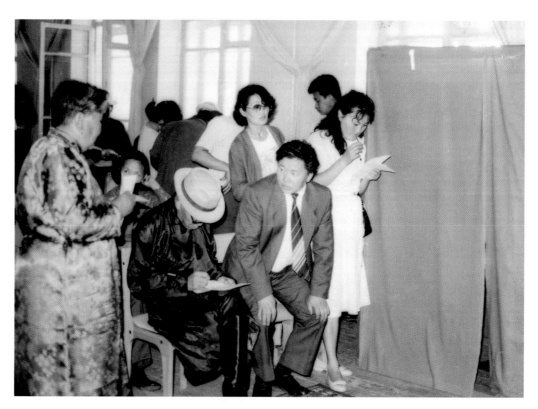

Figure 2.25.
People voting in the
first free election.
(NMMH, July 1990)

25, 1992. The preamble to the constitution set forth the goals of the new Mongolian Republic:

We the people of Mongolia, strengthening the independence and sovereignty of our nation, cherishing human rights, freedoms, justice and national unity, inheriting the traditions of our statehood, history and culture and respecting the common heritage of mankind, aspire to develop a humane, civil and democratic society in our homeland.[46]

In the ten years following the democratic revolution, we have been working to put into effect the principles of the new constitution. This has not been easy, for to form a capitalist, democratic government from a former Communist government, restructuring is necessary for the entire education system, the justice system, the laws concerning property and trade, etc.

The general public also has to learn new ways of thinking and behaving; among them are responsibility for democratic government and economic self-sufficiency. We have had to do this while experiencing the shock of Russian withdrawal of all aid and learning to elicit support from various international governments and agencies. The first few years of the decade were very difficult. Because Russian economic aid had stopped, our factories halted production, trade was interrupted, and markets and stores became empty of goods. Daily necessities were rationed, and even then they were hard to find. The sudden drop in economic performance, inflation, unemployment, foreign debt, and poverty created social resentment. As Mongolians experienced freedom for the first time, they resented any authority. The phrase "Don't you repress me!" became popular, and the question rose whether the country was achieving democracy or anarchy.

But the situation is changing rapidly, and

Figure 2.26 S. Zulsar, a professional throat singer, shares his tradition with public audiences in Ulaanbaatar and around the world. (Joseph Wolek, August 2000)

my country is moving toward its joint goals of establishing democracy and capitalism while preserving national traditions–or reviving them after seventy years of Communist rule! We are no longer dependent on one country. We have established diplomatic relations and trading partnerships with the West as well as China, Japan, South Korea, and our former Communist allies. We have experienced peaceful transitions of power from the MPRP to the Democratic Coalition and back to the MPRP (as of the 1997 presidential election and the 2000 parliamentary election). We have honored the victims of the purges through annual ceremonies and government reparations. We have welcomed national and international non-governmental organizations (NGOs), which are advancing the democratic process, promoting the implementation of human

rights and individual freedoms, expanding political knowledge among citizens, and encouraging political activeness. Pluralism–the right to publicly express one's opinions–and religious freedom have become commonplace. And we are reviving our national traditions in both the public and private arenas. Genghis Khan has become the symbol of our renewed national spirit, for we know that he first gave us our national independence and many of our democratic principles.

In the economic sphere, the initial difficult transition period has given way to markets and department stores filled with imported food, modern bars filled with Mongolian rock band rhythms, and restaurants offering an interesting mix of Mongolian, Western, and Asian cuisine. The capitalist class has been

Figure 2.27.
A ger *with Mercedes Benz, Tuv Aimag.*
(Paula L.W. Sabloff, August 2000)

growing as companies with the multiple shareholders gain in strength and joint venture companies are established. Even the herders are acquiring private cars, their own electric power supply, and new technology. Of course, not all members of our society are succeeding in this new market economy. However, the government continues to work on social security and welfare for the vulnerable strata of society.

Over the course of the last century, Mongolia has achieved its goals, that is, independence and democracy within a market economy structure, but the cost has been high. Many lost their lives; even more suffered from economic, physical and human rights deprivations during the frequent periods of restructuring; and the incessant intergenerational struggle continues. Today my country is more Western than Asian, maintaining a mixture of nomadic and urban lifestyles.

What will our future be? Our population is very young, and I believe that our youth are our strength, for their bright minds and strong bodies grasp the new global society we have struggled to join. My sons' generation studies English, Russian, Japanese, Korean, and German and finds joy in the Internet, Hip Hop music, and basketball. Their peers all over the

Figure 2.28
A pick-up game of basketball with the author's son, Battuulga. (Joseph Wolek, August 2000)

country have a keen awareness of the outside world. But they are also increasing their knowledge of their own proud heritage. I believe that the combination of our youths' interest in international pursuits and awareness of our history and customs will assure Mongolia a proud place in the international community.

NOTES

1. I. M. Maiskii, *Mongolia nakanune revolyutsii* (Mongolia Before the Revolution) (Moscow: Izdatel'stvo Bostochoi Literaturi, 1960), 102-121.

2. Idshinnorov S., *Ulaanbaatar khotin tuukhin khuraangui* (A Brief History of Ulaanbaatar) (Ulaanbaatar: Uria, 1994), 23.

3. Sumya B., *Mongolin nuudelchdiin soyol: orshikhui, es orskhikhui* (The Mongolians' Nomadic Culture: Existence or Non-existence) (Ulaanbaatar: Admon, 1998), 10, 33.

4. Maiskii, *Mongolia,* 300.

5. Jamsran L., *Mongolchuudin sergen mandaltin ekhen,* (The Dawn of the Mongolian Renaissance) (Ulaanbaatar: Soyombo, 1992), 51.

6. *Bogd* means holy, sacred; *gegeen* means an incarnated lama.

7. Jamsran, *Mongolchuudin,* 51.

8. Ibid., 64.

9. Navaannamjil, *Ovgon bicheechiin oguulel* (The Tale of the Old Scribe) (Ulaanbaatar: State Press, 1959).

10. M. Sanjdorj, ed., *Khoridugaar zuunii Mongol* (Twentieth Century Mongolia), trans. Erdem (Ulaanbaatar: Knowledge, 1995), 20.

11. Owen Lattimore, "Mongol-terguuleh oron"

(Mongolia, the Leading Nation) *Khodolmor* 74 (July 4, 1989).

12. *Moskovskaja torgobaja ekspeditsia b Mongolliu b 1910 godu* (Moscow Commercial Expedition in Mongolia 1910) (Moscow: P.P. Rjabushinskii, 1912), 296.

13. Bat-Ochir L., *Tuukhiin Unenii Ereld* (In Search of Historical Truth) (Ulaanbaatar: Urlakh Erdem. Skill to Craft, 1999), 29.

14. Idshinnorov S., *The Flame of Struggle* (Ulaanbaatar: State Press, 1973).

15. Sanjdorj, *Khoridugaar*, 37.

16. *Makhn-in tuukhin chukhal barimtuud* (Official Documents of the MPRP, 1920-1924) (Ulaanbaatar, 1946), 29-33.

17. Luvsandorj P., *BNMAU-in ediin zasgin khogjliin zangilaa asuudluud* (The Intricate Questions of MPR's Economic Development) (Ulaanbaatar: State Press, 1980), 47.

18. Karl Marx (*The German Ideology*, 1845-46) had theorized that humanity passes through five stages in a process of unilineal evolution, a concept that was popular in his day: tribalism, slave holding, feudalism, capitalism, and finally, the Socialist stages (socialism and communism).

19. Gombosuren B., "Bukh tsergin ganjin D. Suhbaatar ulaan tsergin tukhai"(The Military Chief of All Armed Forces D. Suhbaatar on the Question of the Soviet Army), *Zasgin gazrin medee* (The Government News), 11 (1995).

20. Bat-erdene Batbayar, *XX zuunii Mongol: nuudel suudal, garz olz* (Twentieth Century Mongolia: Nomads and Settled, Losses and Gains) (Ulaanbaatar: Ulsiin Gerel Zurgiin Gazar, 1996), 338.

21. Otgonjargal Bat-Ochir, *XX zuuni Mongol dakh uls toriin tuukhen yil yavts* (The Political Actions of Twentieth-century Mongolia) (Ulaanbaatar: State Press, 1966), 61.

22. Batbayar, *XX zuunii Mongol*, 62.

23. Ibid.

24. Lattimore, "Mongol-terguuleh oron."

25. Duinkherjav G., *Davaagin Namsraigin ul torin namtar* (The Political Biography of Davaa Namsrai), trans. Ungut Xevlel (Ulaanbaatar: Colour Printer, 1997), 16.

26. J. Boldbaatar, Ts. Batbayar, and Z. Baasanjav, eds. *Mongol olsiin tuukh* (The History of Mongolia) (Ulaanbaatar: Admon, 1999), 136.

27. *Unuudur* (Today newspaper) 300 (December 5, 2000).

28. Duinkherjav, *Davaagin*, 13.

29. Sanjdorj, *Khoridugaar*, 165.

30. Robert Rupen, *Khoirdugaar zuunii mongolchuud* (Mongols of the Twentieth Century), Mongolian translation by G. Akim (Ulaanbaatar: Monsudar, 2000), 336.

31. *Modern Mongolia* (Mongolian magazine published in Russian), 5 (1960), 40.

32. Idshinnorov, *Ulaanbaatar*, 122.

33. Sumya, ed., *Mongoliin sojolin tuukh* (Mongolian Cultural History) (Ulaanbaatar: Admon, 1999), 235.

34. Actually, spying and other efforts to reveal and punish activists working 'against the Party' continued until the mid-1980s.

35. Sanjdorj, *Khoridugaar*, 68.

36. Boldbaatar et al., *Mongol olsiin tuukh*, (History of the Mongolian People), (Ulaanbaatar: Admon, 1999), 72.

37. Arkadii Stolipin, *Moskva Beejingin zavsar dakh Mongol oron* (Mongolia Between Moscow and Beijing) (Ulaanbaatar: Monsudar, 2000), 132.

38. *National Economy of the MPR* (Ulaanbaatar: State Press, 1986), 14.

39. *Unuudur* (Today), 296 (December 21, 2000).

40. Sumya, *Mongoliin sojolin tuukh*, 235.

41. Badamkhatan, C., "NMAU-in ugsaatni khogjlinjavts" (The Cultural Development of Ethnic Groups in the MPR), *Studia Ethnographica* 7(1) (1982): 16.

42. Sumya, *Mongoliin sojolin tuukh*, 347.

43. From the archives of the National Museum of Mongolian History, A93-13-1 (Ulaanbaatar).

44. Tsogtsaikhan, S., *I Could Not Be Silent* (Ulaanbaatar: State Press, 1991), 50.

45. Dashzeveg X., *The Mongolian National Democratic Party, 1989-1996* (Ulaanbaatar: Interpress, 1998), 21.

46. Alan J. K. Sanders, "Appendix 4: Constitution of Mongolia," *Historical Dictionary of Mongolia*, 272.

Figure 2.29.
Children in racing costume
before the Naadam horse race,
Tuv Aimag. (Joseph Wolek,
August 2000)

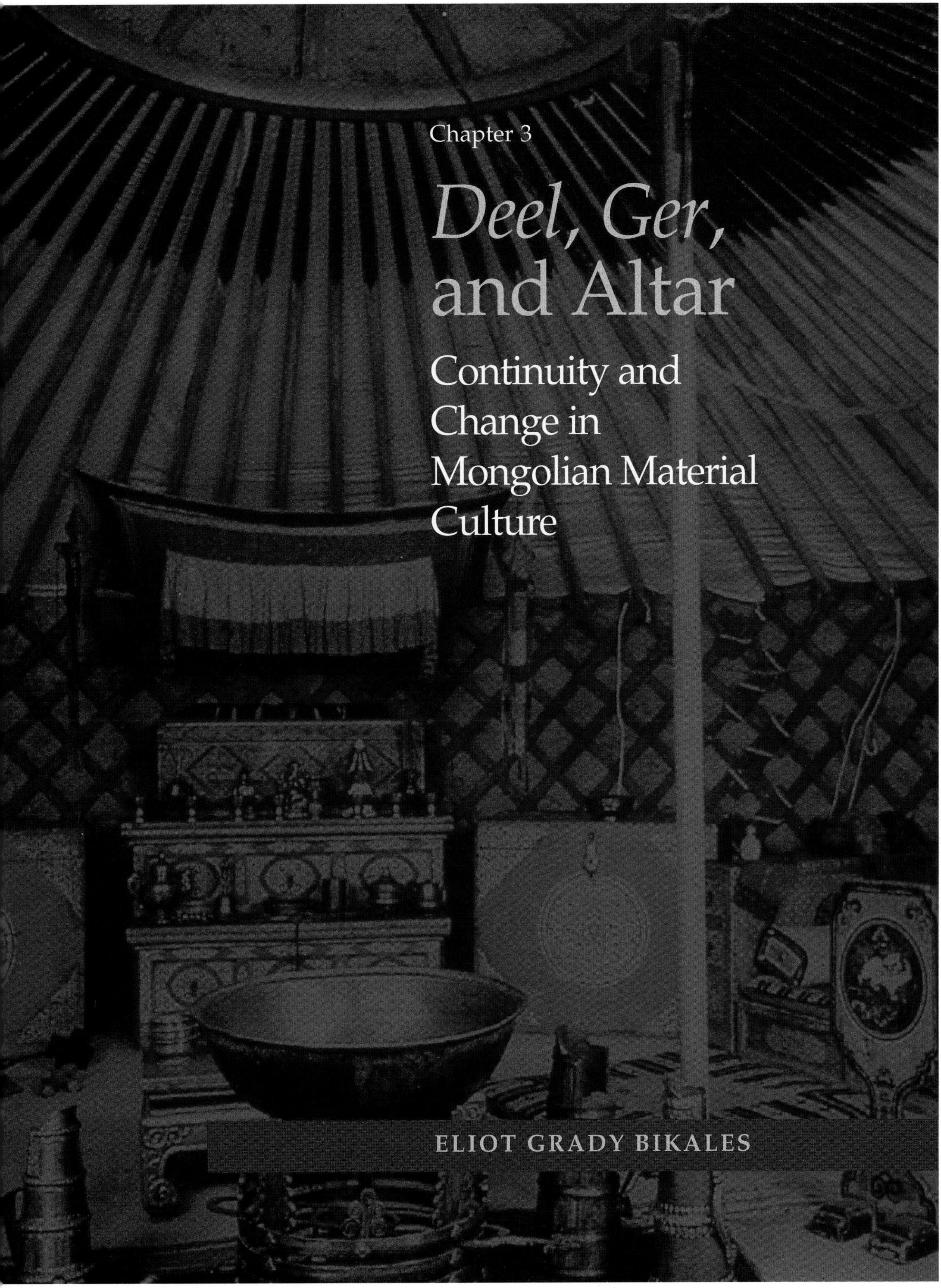

Chapter 3

Deel, Ger, and Altar

Continuity and Change in Mongolian Material Culture

ELIOT GRADY BIKALES

ON A COLD WINTER'S MORN-ING in December 1993, I was staring out my Ulaanbaatar kitchen window at the building across from mine when I spied an old lady stepping out onto her balcony. During Mongolia's long winters, an apartment balcony is used as a natural freezer, and it is not uncommon for several carcasses of cows or sheep to be stored there. I assumed the old lady was going to get some meat to cook. Instead, she dipped a spoon into a small bowl she held and began to sprinkle milk into the air. Intrigued, I set about finding out what exactly she had been doing.

I had been living in Mongolia for about six months and was disappointed that so few traditional rituals could be observed, no doubt related to Mongolia's years of Communist government. Granted, some Mongolians wore their traditional robe, the *deel* (pronounced 'dell'), as daily dress, but there was little color or tradition in everyday life that I could see. This old lady's simple act was a revelation to me–traditional culture had survived communism and was now being practiced openly.

I decided to investigate, and thus began my metamorphosis from a Chinese art historian to an amateur Mongolian ethnographer. I quickly learned that the restrictions of nomadic life dictated that everyday objects doubled as works of art. Clothing, furniture, and utensils all bear the signs of this artistry. This high-level union of art and practical objects allowed me to satisfy my two areas of interest. As I later discovered, my training in Chinese art history proved invaluable.

I also learned that the changes in political systems during the twentieth century–from Manchu Dynasty feudalism to Soviet-inspired communism and finally to market-economy democracy–greatly affected the material culture of the Mongolians. The style and material used in clothing, ornamentation, housing, and furniture have been greatly modified under different governments.

Clothing and Personal Ornament

In 1994-5, as an Assistant Curator at the NMMH, the first project I helped with was the installation of the Costume Gallery. In the ear-ly twentieth century, Mongolia had about twenty ethnic groups, from the Kazakhs in the northwest to the Uzemchin in the southeast. Originally, each had its own distinct style of dress, boots, and hat, and a large selection can be seen in the gallery. The largest ethnic group is the Halh.

It is important to note that there is no history of weaving in Mongolia. Early clothing was made from animal skins. The Mongolian steppe and forests provided a wide variety of fur, which was used for trim on hats and as lining for *deel*s. Cloth was one of the primary reasons Mongolians traded with and raided other civilizations. The majority of fabrics used in Halh clothing came from China, but Tibetan silks (made from silk threads imported from China) were most highly prized.

The *Deel*, Traditional Dress of the Mongols

The *deel*, which is still worn by men, women, and children, is a caftan-like garment with buttons at the collar, right side of the chest, the right underarm, and down the right side. In the summer, people wear a cotton or silk *deel* while in the winter they wear a fur-lined or cotton-padded *deel*. A common sight in summer, when a *deel* can be too hot for comfort, is a man with one arm slipped out of his *deel*, revealing an imported T-shirt underneath.

Three main features of the *deel* apply to all ethnic groups and time periods. Its design allows maximum flexibility for horse-riding nomads; its ample size allows it to be used as a covering for nights spent on the open steppe; and it can hold all the things a person needs in his or her daily activities.[1]

While Mongols often wear the *deel* today–as daily wear or festive dress in Ulaanbaatar as well as in the countryside–it dates back at least to the Hunnu Empire (fourth century BCE to first century CE). Mongolians claim that during the Manchu reign (seventeenth to early twentieth century), they were ordered to wear *deel*s with very long sleeves. In China, this sleeve style dates back to those worn by dancing girls in the Tang Dynasty (eighth century). Many Mongolians like to say the Chinese forced this style on them in order to make

Figure 3.1. People still wear their deel*s as everyday dress in the city, Ulaanbaatar. (Joseph Wolek, September 2000)*

Figure 3.2. Brothers in their deel, *Ih Huree. (NMMH, early 20th century)*

their work more difficult, but generally only the ceremonial *deel*s have the very long sleeves.

The sleeves of a *deel* end in a graceful cuff sometimes referred to as a horse-hoof cuff because of its shape. Found on normal-length sleeves, these cuffs offer protection from the elements. They fold down to cover the hands, especially important when riding a horse in the cold winter.

Another Manchu influence on the Mongolian costume is the high collar found on the *deel*s to this day. The traditional Mongolian *deel*, called *huv engert*, had no collar. This collarless style dates back to the Hunnu period as evidenced in the robe found in a Hunnu era tomb on Noyon Uul (Mount Noyon) in Tuv Aimag. The 'imposition' of a Mandarin collar on the Mongolian costume is actually beneficial, since the collar provides added protection from the cold wind.

Halh Men's Traditional Clothing

By the early part of the twentieth century, traditional Halh Mongols wore a *deel* with a Mandarin collar covered by a short vest. Underneath they wore a special kind of boot with the *deel*. These are very distinctive as they have raised ornamental designs and up-turned toes. One theory about the up-turned toe shape is that Mongolians, who are Buddhists, do not want to disturb the earth, and a raised-toe boot will not kick up dirt. Another theory is that the up-turned toe keeps the foot in stirrups better than an ordinary boot. Traditional Halh boots are not very easy to walk in, and it seems plausible that they were designed for people who rode more than walked. As with many aspects of any culture, Buddhist interpretations may have been added at a later date when the original intention of the design was forgotten.

Both men's and women's leather boots have raised leather designs. Design patterns are cut into wood, and wet leather is then pressed into the indentations. Some boots are embroidered instead. The most common pattern is the *ulzii*, or never-ending knot, symbolizing longevity.

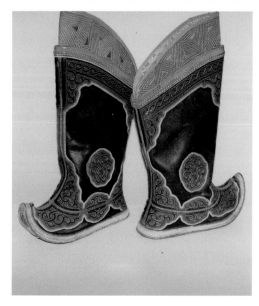

Figure 3.3. Boots of a traditional Halh man. (NMMH)

A felt lining extends above the top of the boot, and the visible section is covered in fabric that often sports beautiful embroidery.

A sash, or *buus* (*bus*), is considered an essential part of the Mongolian costume. The length of the sash varies, but typically a man's is approximately fifteen to eighteen feet long, while a woman's is nine to twelve feet. The man's fabric is folded into a wide band, which is tightly wrapped just under the natural waistline. This tight sash is said to keep one's inner organs in place while riding across the rocky Mongolian steppe. Many superstitions surround the sash. For example, it is a bad omen to leave it tied somewhere. If one finds one's sash still tied, the owner must approach an older person within three days and ask him/her to untie it. The older person then asks what has been happening in the past three days and makes appropriate wishes for the sash owner. Also, it is not appropriate to give one's sash to someone else, although it is becoming acceptable to give it to a foreigner.

Men suspend various bags and implements needed during the day from the sash. These include a knife (with or without chopsticks, which were introduced during the Manchu era), a rectangular pouch folded over the sash that holds a snuff bottle, another pouch for a drinking bowl, and a flint and steel set (the Mongolian equivalent of the Swiss Army knife) for starting fires. Additional storage is created inside the *deel* above the sash, between the shoulder and underarm buttons.

To top off this outfit, a man wears a four-sided, tall pointed hat. In Mongolian culture, it is considered polite to leave one's hat on when entering a *ger* or apartment. When it is time to remove the hat, it is treated with great respect and is not casually left lying around. In a *ger*, Mongolians place their hats facing toward the south (the door) on a trunk in the area farthest from the door. There are also certain rules for treating a hat. One should never point one's feet toward a hat and never place a hat with its opening upwards. Mongolians do not exchange hats with one another, and traditionally they do not throw them away. However, with the influx of cheap Chinese goods that flood the Mongolian market today, most hats are bought rather than made at home, and they do not last very long.

Figure 3.4. The implements worn by a Halh man in the early twentieth century: knife, chopsticks, and a flint and steel set. (NMMH)

MEN'S CLOTHING DURING COMMUNISM

The change in societal structure from Manchu Dynasty feudalism with its strict class hierarchy (see Chapter 2) to Soviet-linked communism naturally resulted in changes in the traditional costume. Tall Russian black leather boots replaced the Mongolian up-turned toe boots for everyday use. Leather belts became popular, replacing the sash, and vests went out of style. Long sleeves and horse-hoof cuffs disappeared from the *deel*, along with men's elaborate hats. In the 1920s Natsagdorj, a famous author, started a fashion trend, which still con

tinues today: he topped his *deel* with a felt fedora.

In 1938, Stalin decreed that national costumes were no longer acceptable, and it was forbidden to wear a *deel* to an office job. Two prominent scholars, Rinchen and Ts. Damdin suren, defied this decree and continued to wear *deel*s in public.

MEN'S CLOTHING TODAY

In 1990, the president of the new democratic country, Ochirbat, wore a beautiful white *deel* with dark brown appliqué trim to his inaugu-

Figure 3.5. A modern man wearing his Communist-era outfit: cotton deel, *traditional hat, and Roman medals. (Joseph Wolek, September 2000)*

Figure 3.6, right. Men's clothing varies according to the occasion and mood of the wearer. Here city and country-side friends await the horse race at the Tuv Aimag Naadam. (Joseph Wolek, August 2000)

ration. In addition to signaling that Mongolians could freely wear traditional clothes now that Communism had ended, this ceremonial *deel* also exhibited the continuing tradition of costume design and execution.

While it is not uncommon today to see a man in a *deel*, businessmen generally wear suits and ties. Teenagers prefer jeans, T-shirts, and baseball hats. In the countryside, a *deel* worn with a baseball hat–often with the letters LA or NY appliquéd over the brim–is very common.

Traditional Halh Women's Clothing

Under Manchu times at the beginning of the twentieth century, what a woman wore was dictated by her marital status. Before her marriage, a young girl wore a simple *deel* with a belt. Her hair was braided and she wore a rounded hat called a *toortsog*.

Figure 3.7. Halh women of the wealthy or princely class, Ih Huree. (NMMH, early twentieth century)

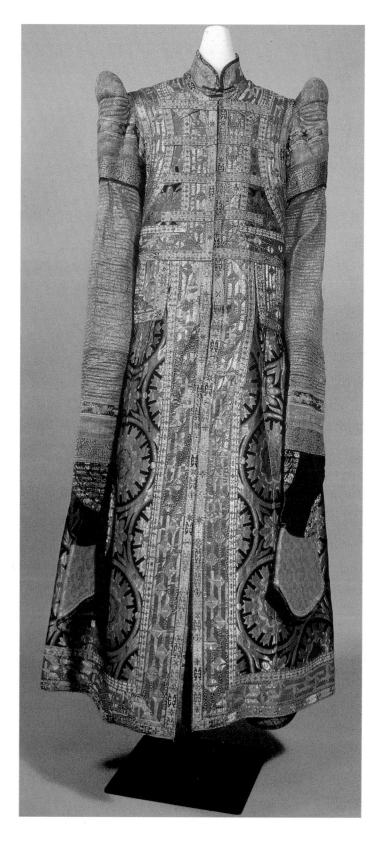

Marriage imposed a striking change in costume. When a girl became engaged, the groom's family would bring her a gift of cloth, an example of its value. Then, as part of her dowry, the bride's parents would prepare clothes for her. They would make at least ten *deel*s and present them to the bride on her wedding day before she left her childhood home. That day she was taken on horseback to the family *ger* of the groom. On this ride, she was covered with a red cloth so that she could not see where she was going and therefore would not know how to return home if she became unhappy.

Upon arrival at her new home, the bride dressed in an elaborate outfit. First she put on a sashless *deel*. A Mongolian word for wife is "sashless." The lack of a sash was both symbolic and practical. By giving up her sash, the bride was showing submission, a visible sign that she was bound by and to her husband. On the practical side, a sashless outfit was more comfortable during pregnancy.

On top of the *deel* the bride wore a vest that was practically as long as her *deel*. Since the lack of a sash prevented her from carrying implements for daily use (as she did before marriage), chatelaines hung off the sides of her vest. A chatelaine is a set of chains on which a woman would hang various utensils such as tweezers, an ear pick, or a case for needles. In some cases, symbolic ornaments replaced the implements, and the chatelaine lost its utilitarian function.

Now that she was getting married, the bride exchanged her rounded hat for a tall, pointed one. The most striking part of her outfit, however, was her elaborate headdress. A tale the explorer Henning Haslund heard on his 1927-30 expedition concerning the origins of this unique headdress says that the Halh Mongols are descendants of a cow[2]; therefore Halh women fashion their hair in imitation of a cow's horns and pad the shoulders of their clothing to resemble a cow's protruding shoulder blades. Martha Boyer, a jewelry expert, repeats this legendary origin of the Mongolians and the Halh hairstyle in her book, *Mongol Jewelry*.[3]

The story about the cow strikes me as very odd. First, Halh Mongols believe that they are descended from a blue-gray wolf and a beautiful deer, as recorded in the opening of *The*

Secret History of the Mongols.[4] Second, it is the Buriad, not the Halh, who believe they are descended from a blue cow. It would be useful to know the tribal affiliation of the Mongolian prince who spoke with Haslund.

My colleagues at the National Museum of Mongolian History do not agree with the cow story, and they directed me to a different tale about the origin of the Halh woman's headdress, called "The Crow Fears the Garuda." In order to peck away at the Mongolian family's spirit, the Manchu's introduced a fireplace with four prongs that look like crows' beaks. The Mongolians thought of various ways to frighten away the crows and at last came upon the Garuda, the mythical king of the birds. Because the person constantly beside the fireplace is a married woman, the Mongolians devised a hairstyle for her that resembled the wings of the Garuda. When the woman wears this hairstyle, the crow, fearing the Garuda, cannot cause any harm. The raised shoulder pads, stuffed with starched felt or wool, are said to resemble the Garuda's hunched shoulders. In reality, these help support the weight of the headdress.

This tale is interesting for its anti-Manchu or -Chinese sentiment and its Buddhist overtones, as the Garuda was introduced into Mongolia along with Buddhism in the seventeenth century. The distinctive Halh married woman's headdress dates from the eighteenth century. As chronicled by the Mongolian scholars H. Nyambuu and J. Tsevegsuren the 'crow-beak' fireplace also first appeared in the eighteenth century.[5] Thus the connection between the Garuda and women's hairstyle may be plausible. However charming this well-known tale is, a definitive answer to the origin of this hairstyle remains elusive.

On a traditional Halh girl's wedding day, her hair was combed out, parted down the middle, and glued into the wing-like style of the Garuda with congealed animal fat. Double-sided barrettes encrusted with semiprecious stones helped to keep her hair in place. The remaining hair was braided and encased in braid sheaths of decorated brocade. Traditionally, a woman's beauty was judged only by the length of her hair, and braid sheaths ensured at least the appearance of long hair. (For a man, the broader the back of the neck, the more handsome he was.)

On top of her head and lying rather low across her forehead, a married Halh woman wore a metal skullcap. The traditional skullcap has a hole in the center, which some Mongolian scholars believe to be the remnant of a style of hat popular in Kubilai Khan's court in China. Court women of that era wore a round cloth hat called a *bahtah* (*bakhtakh*), which had a large cylindrical decoration rising from the center of the cap. This piece could be removed when needed, for example when going through a low *ger* door, and reinserted quickly. In turn, this hat was styled on hats worn by some women in Genghis Khan's time.

Because the glued hair, skullcap, barrettes, braid sheaths, and hat could weigh as much as twenty-five pounds, women could not wear this style continuously. However, since setting it up was labor-intensive, custom dictated that once their hair was done up, they would leave it in place for three to four weeks. The result was often an indentation in the forehead when they finally took the ornaments off.

Women did up their hair for ceremonies and other special occasions, such as *Tsagaan Sar*, the Lunar New Year. In some regions in Mongolia, one woman from a *ger* settlement would dress up in her finery to lead the procession of families and animals to a new campsite. This was still practiced in the early 1900s. At the turn of the twentieth century, women started using wigs of yak hair wrapped around thin boards to simplify the adornment process.

WOMEN'S CLOTHING DURING COMMUNISM

The Communist dress code did not permit such blatant gender or class discrimination as seen in the early twentieth century Halh costume. Signals of class differentiation and ornamentation were against the concept of economic egalitarianism, the core of Communist doctrine. The headdress that was given as part of a girl's dowry in pre-Communist times naturally reflected the economic condition of her family. During communism, dowries were discouraged and the authorities confiscated many of these headdresses. Some women turned their headdress sets into other pieces of jewelry or drinking bowls so that they could pass their precious jewelry on to their daugh-

Figure 3.9. A young nomad woman wears the same clothing as women did in the Communist era: plain cotton deel *and headscarf, Hentii Aimag. (Joseph Wolek, August 2000)*

ters, but of course they did so under great secrecy.

Under the Communist government, women's *deel*s resembled men's. Sashless *deel*s disappeared, and all women wore belts, often made of leather. Russian-style kerchiefs often replaced hats.

WOMEN'S CLOTHING TODAY

In today's democracy, married women's *deel*s do not differ in style from unmarried women's or men's. All wear belts. The preferred fashion for women is a thin, silver- or gold- colored belt. Women of all ages and marital statuses wear the round hat that had been worn by traditional Halh unmarried women in Manchu times.

After the fall of communism in 1990, many young people began wearing their first *deel*s. In the spring, female university students wear *deel*s to graduation ceremonies and can be seen having their photos taken in colorful silk *deel*s in Suhbaatar Square, Ulaanbaatar. The original *deel* without a Manchu collar has also regained

*Figure 3.10.
City women wear a mixture of styles to celebrate a wedding, Ulaanbaatar. (Joseph Wolek,*

popularity, and people proudly point out that it is the true Mongolian style. Traditional clothing is yet another aspect of Mongolian culture that has survived communism.

Children's Clothing

Like adult clothing, early twentieth-century children's clothing varied from one ethnic group to another. Children's clothing was also affected by communist restrictions. During communism, children were required to wear uniforms to school, and the girls were required to adorn their hair with oversized chiffon 'socialist bows.' Girls who did not do this, or did a messy job, were punished at school. Since democracy was instituted in 1990, school uniforms were less commonly seen. However the current MPRP government is re-instituting uniforms.

The first time a child dons a *deel*, a special ceremony is held. According to tradition, the child's first *deel* is sewn during sunrise. Parents consult Buddhist monks to determine the most auspicious day and time for cutting the

Figure 3.11. Students wore school uniforms in Communist times. (NMMH, 1960s)

Figure 3.12. A little boy in a deel, *Tuv Aimag Naadam. (Joseph Wolek, August 2000)*

fabric, sewing the *deel*, attaching the buttons, and making the sash.[6] When ready for the ceremony, the family clears the *ger* fire, and the child's mother helps him or her put on the *deel*, anointing it with animal fat such as a piece of sheep's tail or a milk product, while reciting the following, and tugging on the appropriate parts of the *deel* as they are mentioned:

Have a long life and live happily!
May many foals and colts step forth from
the lower front of your *deel*,
And many sheep and goats from the lower
back of your *deel*.
You are eternal,
Your possessions are mortal.
This year you wear cotton;
We hope next year you will wear expensive
cloth.
May the inside of your *deel* give oil and fat!
May you grow through the roof ring [of a
ger] and wear a silk *deel*.

Today, Western-style clothing for boys and girls predominates, although Mongolians do not adhere to the 'pink for girls, blue for boys' custom that many Westerners follow. However, the practice of swaddling newborns in quilts continues, especially in winter. Traditionally, when babies were born in a *ger*, they were immediately wrapped (swaddled) in a sheepskin so tightly that their arms and legs could not move. Today, between 95 to 97 percent of women give birth in hospitals, where their newborns are swaddled. A swaddled baby cannot roll off a bed, does not risk dying of SIDS, and is warmly protected against the elements. However, the negative side of this practice is that babies who are swaddled too much do not get enough sunshine or exercise and so they develop rickets. The rickets usually disappear as the toddlers play in the sunshine.

Ornamentation

Ornamentation raises the everyday object to a work of art, be it jewelry or utensil. Silver is the most commonly used metal for this purpose. While silver is abundant in Mongolia, most of that used in ornaments before the advent of communism was imported from China. Silver ingots were melted down and hammered into extremely thin sheets from which jewelers cut various patterns using birch-bark stencils. On occasion, they sewed coins onto clothing, which was particularly popular on married women's braid sheaths. Artisans did not melt down silver coins, as the silver content was not pure enough for jewelry.

Halh Mongols often preferred semiprecious stones interspersed with the silver work. The three most popular stones were turquoise, pearl, and coral. Turquoise came from Mongolia, while the other two were imported via the

Figure 3.13. The tradtional headdress of a Halh woman shows the use of semi-precious stones in the design. (NMMH)

caravans that traveled the Silk Roads. People also used these stones for medicinal purposes, especially as a remedy for poisoning, which was a popular way of doing away with enemies. Perhaps then these stones served a dual purpose–ornamentation and protection.

Halh clothing and accessories widely incorporated embroidery and appliqué into the finished pieces. However, some of the finest work remaining today was reserved for snuff bottle pouches. Tiny beads of pearl or coral were often sewn onto the appliqué designs. Mongolia's unique contribution to religious appliqué was the addition of these beads.

The Mongol's disdain for anything Chinese was in contradiction to the widespread use of Chinese symbolism on everyday objects. The use of these symbols is not surprising, given that most artisans were Chinese or of Chinese descent; they moved from *ger* settlement to *ger*

settlement as need demanded. A frequent symbol was the Chinese character *shou* (Mongolian: *lanz*), which means longevity. Dragons also are abundant, especially on the handles of the Mongolian teapot called the *dombo*. Tibetan designs such as the king's earrings (Mongolian: *Haan Buguivch*) and the queen's earrings (Mongolian: *Hatan Suih*) were popular and are still the traditional design for wedding rings. These designs are still seen on the gates of *ger* "suburbs" in Ulaanbaatar.

The Mongolian *Ger*

The *ger*, still home to almost half of today's Mongolians, is the ideal dwelling for nomads. It can be broken down or reassembled in less than an hour and transported easily by cart or camel back. During communism, when gasoline was abundant and subsidized by the government, trucks were used more often than carts. Today, many herders are reverting to yak or camel carts to move their *ger*s. The *ger*'s aerodynamic design allows it to remain standing even in the worst windstorms,

Figure 3.14, below. A man holding his snuff bottle outside his ger, *Tuv Aimag. (Joseph Wolek, Agust 2000)*

Figure 3.15, below right. Nomads moving their ger *in a yak-drawn cart, Hentii Aimag. (Paula L.W. Sabloff, August 2000)*

although flash floods have been known to sweep *ger*s away.

From the outside, a *ger* looks small and gives the impression that it is very dark inside. However, the inside of a *ger* is surprisingly bright and spacious. The size of a *ger* is measured by the number of collapsible, latticework wall sections made of branches or wooden slats. The standard *ger* has five walls, but there are also four-, six-, or even eight-walled *ger*s. These can be further subdivided into 'large-wall' and 'small-wall' *ger*s, depending on the length of each lattice wall. Although I live in the city, I own a *ger* in the countryside. It is a standard five-wall *ger* and is approximately seventeen feet in diameter. One of my Mongolian friends lives in a six-wall *ger* in which he has an upright piano. In the summer when it is too hot to light a fire in the *ger*, it is not uncommon to find very small *ger*s of two or three walls used as a kitchen. Of course, cooking can also be done al fresco.[7]

To assemble a *ger*, the family first inserts two wall sections into holes on either side of the low door. Next someone lashes the remaining wall sections to the first two, forming a circle.

Figure 3.16. Setting up the ger's roof ring, Hentii Aimag. (Paula L.W. Sabloff, August 2000)

Once the walls are set up, one person holds up the two poles that support the roof ring, while others insert the roof poles. One end of these fits into square holes carved into the roof ring's outer circle, and the other end rests on top of the lattice walls. People with strong fingers secure the roof poles to the lattice walls with a small loop of rope traditionally made of horsehair. A standard five-wall *ger* has eighty-one roof poles. Mongols consider nine, and any derivative of it, an auspicious number for poles or anything else.

Once all the roof poles are secured, the family or friends surround the outer walls and roof with a felt covering, leaving the roof ring uncovered. They then cover the felt with either a canvas covering or a waterproof lining topped by a white cotton cover. My *ger*'s waterproof lining is made of old plastic milk bags sewn together, showing the resourceful-ness and economy of the original owners. In summer, which can be as hot as the winter is cold, the *ger* coverings can be raised about eight inches from the bottom to allow ventilation.

To make sure that the covering does not blow away, people tie horsehair or synthetic ropes around the *ger* from the left side of the door to the right. Finally, they tie a square piece of cloth, folded into a triangle, over the roof ring on the outside of the *ger*. This can be unfolded, by means of ropes, to cover the entire roof ring in case of rain or snow, making the *ger* noticeably darker. Many families today put plastic or glass in the roof ring so that they do not lose the light when weather is bad.

In Mongolia, the *ger* door always faces south. This allows as much sunlight as possible to enter the *ger* and also offers protection against strong winds that blow from the north.

Figure 3.17. Putting on the ger's *felt lining before the canvas covering, Hentii Aimag. (Paula L.W. Sabloff, August 2000)*

In the summer, it is common to have no flooring. In the winter, most use a wooden floor with carpets on top. Some use a linoleum-covered floor, as people reserve carpets for decoration on *ger* walls, like paintings in Western homes. They depict anything from a Mongolian landscape to Pope John Paul II or the Mona Lisa, an example of the liberation of artistic subject matter after communism.

In the past, the *ger* door was simply an extra piece of felt. This evolved into a wooden door. Although some *ger* doors may have a glass window, glass was not very common. During winter, Mongolians sometimes add a cover of felt or padded cloth to the door. Mongolians are careful not to step on the sill of a door, as spirits are said to reside there, but unknowing foreigners are not scorned if they do so.

The stove sits in the center of the *ger*. The fuel used for the fire depends on the resources of the area. In the steppe zones, where wood is scarce, children and women collect dung to burn. Even today, children with baskets on their backs and rakes in hand, combing the steppe for dung, are a common sight. In summer, people burn a small piece of dung outside the *ger* door to keep bugs out.

Figure 3.18. Tying on the ger's roof cover with camel hair ropes, Hentii Aimag. (Paula L.W. Sabloff, August 2000)

EARLY HISTORY OF THE *GER*

The *ger* dates back at least 2,000 years, although its origins remain obscure. Two theories predominate. The first is that it evolved from the tipi, which still is home to the *Tsataan*, or Reindeer People, in northern Mongolia. The second holds that it developed from the dugout dwelling, which dates to somewhere between 7000 and 2000 BCE. This type of dwelling gradually rose aboveground. Once the basic circular shape was set, some changes in structure occurred, most notably in the angle of the roof poles and the structure of the roof ring. The Mongolian *ger* has remained largely the same as the prototype.

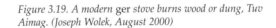

Figure 3.19. A modern ger *stove burns wood or dung, Tuv Aimag. (Joseph Wolek, August 2000)*

THE EARLY TWENTIETH-CENTURY *GER*

Figure 3.20 shows a national treasure in the National Museum of Mongolian History and a

Figure 3.20.
The exterior of the
National Museum's
early twentieth-
century ger.
(NMMH, Hessig
and Mueller, 1989)

Figure 3.21.
The interior of the
National Museum's
early twentieth-
century ger.
(NMMH, Hessig
and Mueller, 1989)

good example of how *ger*s were designed at the beginning of the last century.

The interior is strictly arranged. The roof ring, which also acts as a sundial, divides the *ger* into twelve sections, named according to the twelve animals of the Asian zodiac. Each section is home to a particular item of furniture. A broader division of the *ger* interior has three sections–the man's to the left, the woman's to the right, and the *hoimor* (*khoimor*), or place of honor, at the north side. The host is usually seated on the eastern side of the *hoimor* and the guest to his right. The hostess's place is near the hearth. Children sit near her by the door.

Upon entering a *ger*, one should always move in a clockwise fashion. Immediately to the left of the door is the space traditionally reserved for the sack, made from two goat or sheepskins, used in fermenting mare's milk (or camel's milk in the Gobi Desert). This national drink of Mongolia is called *airag* (airak) in Mongolian and koumiss in the West. Both *airag* and unfermented mare's milk are believed to have curative properties.

The churning stick used to mix the old cul-

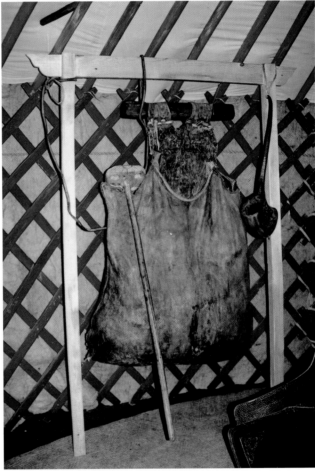

Figure 3.22. An early twentieth-century skin bag that holds airag *(fermented mare's milk, about the strength of beer). Evaporation keeps the* airag *cold and fresh. (NMMH, photograph courtesy of De Nieuwe Kirk, 1999)*

ture into the new mare's milk has a long wooden handle with an inverted bowl-shaped piece of wood containing several holes at one end. It is an important article for nomads of Central Asia; in fact, Bishkek, the capital of Kirgizstan, means "churning stick."

Continuing clockwise, the next section of the *ger* is for the saddle, when not in use. The distinctive Mongolian saddle has a wooden seat, which rises high in both the front and the back. The seat itself is covered with felt or cloth, and its edges are sometimes trimmed in bone that has been soaked in yogurt to make it pliable, and the rest is painted. The saddle is decorated with silver ornaments known as 'whites.' Twelve whites are attached if the owner can afford it. Some of the whites have long leather straps used for tying bags onto the saddle. The leather parts of the saddle are

Figure 3.23. An early twentieth-century saddle. (NMMH)

decorated with raised leather designs, made in the same fashion as those on leather boots.

Next is a wooden bed, which effectively doubles as a couch. Its back is sectioned so that it fits into the *ger* wall. The two 'armrests' contain built-in drawers–another example of the economical use of space.

To the right of the bed is a chest or trunk, which usually comes in pairs that flank the altar. It is used to store clothing, bedding, or other possessions. Since a *ger* does not allow the luxury of closets or wardrobes, these chests are packed tightly. A Mongolian proverb admonishes people, "Instead of begging from your neighbor, look inside your own trunk."

Directly opposite the door is the space of honor reserved for the altar with a canopy above. The wooden altar in Figure 3.22 consists of three pieces stacked together, a common formation. Altars of wealthier families are often carved, while altars in the *ger* of ordinary families have painted designs, in freehand or stenciled or both.

Just as the size, shape, and decoration of altars vary according to the economic situation of the family, so do the religious objects they hold. The three-sectioned altar displays a Tibetan Buddhist *sutra* (*sudar*), or book, on the top shelf. In the early 1900s, the pages of Mongolian books were printed with wooden blocks in Tibetan style; that is, the leaves were not bound together but were wrapped in a cloth, as is the *sutra* displayed here.

The two lower sections hold numerous ritual objects. Among these are the bell and *ochir* (Tibetan: *dorj*), or "thunderbolt." While chanting, a lama holds the bell in his left hand and the *ochir* in his right. A gilt bronze statue of a Buddha is also displayed on this altar. Other objects include a silver *stupa*, oil lamps, an incense holder, and a ritual teapot.

To the right of the altar is a chest or trunk matching the one on the left-hand side of the altar and a second bed. Between the bed and door is the woman's side of the *ger*, containing the "kitchen" shelves and utensils. The shelves hold a variety of pots, while various utensils are hung from the lattice walls or tucked into the roof poles. The most common platter is a round or oblong wooden board for serving meat. It often has legs and "ears." On holidays such as *Tsagaan Sar* a boiled sheep carcass is displayed in a specified arrangement

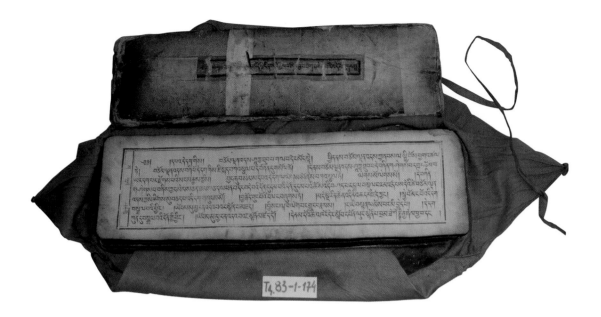

Figure 3.24, above. An early twentieth-century sutra, or Tibetan Buddhist religious book. (NMMH, photograph courtesy of De Nieuwe Kerk, 1999)

Figure 3.25, right. A Buddhist altar statue of Zonhor, in gilt brass. (NMMH)

on the platter. The sheep's tail must face the door so that it is the first thing a visitor sees. A sheep stores the bulk of its fat in its tail, and a sheep with a fat tail will survive the winter well. Mongolians love to eat this fat, and they offer the fat tail to guests as a sign of respect.

In the center of the *ger*, directly underneath the roof ring, is the cooking fire. In the early twentieth century, a type of iron hearth called *tulga* was used. A large cauldron is placed on top of the *tulga*, and the smoke from the fire rises through the roof ring. The *tulga* is the symbol of the home, and many aspects of fire worship, with which it is closely associated, survive today. For example, after a sheep is killed, a piece of the tail fat is tossed onto the fire. Mongolians also never burn trash in the *tulga* or stove; this is tantamount to insulting the host's family, as the *tulga* is also known as *aavin golomt*, or parental hearth.

Between the fireplace and the altar are a low table and stools painted with various patterns. In the early twentieth century red-painted furniture predominated, but by the end of the century, a bright orange was preferred. Ordinary, everyday bowls and pots are found on or around this table. The most common vessel was the *dombo*, or teapot. Made of wood, copper, or silver, the *dombo* comes in various sizes. The largest, the horse *dombo*, was used in monasteries to serve the lamas' tea.

Tea and other drinks are drunk out of bowls, most of which are made of wood and silver. The finest were produced in Dariganga, in southeastern Mongolia, during the late nineteenth to early twentieth centuries, and they are decorated with intricate designs in Mongolian symbols. Men preferred to carry their silver-lined bowl with them for a very practical reason. It is said that when a poisoned liquid is poured into a silver vessel, the silver changes color and the owner knows not to drink the liquid offered.

A custom that still can be seen today is related to this. Like the tales about the Mongolian headdress, this too comes from Manchu times when poisoning was rife: A group of Mongolians were invited to a dinner with the Manchu emperor of China. A man named Yadam, who wore a big silver ring on his ring finger, was among the invited guests. When their host offered the group vodka in a bowl not made of silver, Yadam dipped his ring finger in the vodka and flicked the liquid into the air three times while saying, "For the eternal heaven, for the earth, and for our people." While he was doing this, the vodka dripped down onto his ring, and the ring immediately turned dark, revealing that the drink was poisoned. Thus Yadam saved his fellow countrymen, and to this day the ring finger is known as *yadam*.

CHANGES DURING COMMUNISM

During the Communist era, people began to accumulate more goods and needed more storage space. They started buying suitcases to hold their possessions, stacking them on the wooden chests on either side of the north wall. The suitcases were often covered with embroidered cloths. It was also common to see a hand-cranked sewing machine on one of the trunks, generally the one to the right of the altar, on the woman's side of the *ger*. And metal camp beds that were easily collapsible and easy to move often replaced the traditional wooden beds.

In Communist times the altar disappeared from the *ger* because it was forbidden under the regime. The space reserved for the altar became the site for a Communist showcase. The altar itself was replaced by a chest in which everyday objects were stored. A radio was proudly displayed on top of the chest. The most famous radio was the Russian-made 'Motherland' brand of the 1960s. Where pic-

Figure 3.26. A Communist-era "altar" holds family photographs and honors, ceramic horses, and a radio. (Joseph Wolek, September 2000)

tures of the Bogd Khan once hung, a triptych of a mirror flanked by two frames appeared. These frames held family photographs, certificates, or awards received by members of the family, or photographs of the current leader of Mongolia.

Also found on the chest were productivity awards earned by family members. These awards came in the form of medals and silver statues of the five snouted animals–the camel, horse, cattle (cow or yak), sheep, and goat–that had been domesticated in Mongolia for centuries, as evidenced in early cave paintings in Western Mongolia. While Asian agricultural societies have the five grains (rice, barley, millet, beans, and foxtail millet), the mainstay of the Mongolian domesticates is the five snouted animals.

GERS IN THE DEMOCRATIC ERA

Gers have not changed much since Mongolia became a democratic country. The arrangement of objects is the same as it was at the beginning of the twentieth century. The biggest change is found in the altar/showcase directly opposite the door. While the altar had totally disappeared during communism, it has made a comeback as a combination altar/showcase, and items displayed are no longer limited to those manufactured in the Soviet Union and its satellites. SONY and Panasonic have replaced the 'Motherland' radio. Pictures of the Dalai Lama supplant photos of former communist leaders. Family photographs remain, but newspaper or magazine photos of international stars often accom-

Figure 3.27. These silver statues of the domesticated animals are awards given to herders for producing large herds in Communist times. Award statues, buckets, and medals distinguished hard workers from others, not salary differences. (NMMH)

Figure 3.28. Democracy period ger *altar (Joseph Wolek, September 2000)*

pany them. Michael Jordan is big here. Another big innovation is the beginning of portable solar panels and even windmills, allowing some *ger* owners to generate electricity for television.

Today, most *ger*s have two beds, placed across from each other. Many visitors are surprised to see just two or three beds in a *ger* for a large family. Family members may double up and some will sleep on the floor on blankets. And *ger* families have sets of imported (mostly Chinese) porcelain rice bowls rather than having people carry their bowls with them. Actually, an inventory of a modern Mongolian *ger* would reveal many imported objects, from the children's Chinese-made clothing to Czech cookies and Japanese electronic equipment.

While the material possessions of Mongolians changed considerably during the twentieth century, the landscape outside the *ger* has not. When I step outside my *ger*, near the Haan Hentii Protected Area in Tuv Aimag, the incomparable beauty of the Mongolian landscape never fails to amaze me. I know that although communism could change schooling, religious beliefs, and daily life, it could not break the Mongolians' love of nature and the rituals associated with it.

This idea leads us back to the beginning of this chapter. Just what was that woman doing on her balcony that cold winter morning? In the course of my studies, I learned that she was offering the first milk of the day to the spirits–spirits that preceded Tibetan Buddhism in this beautiful land. I learned that the tradi-

Figure 3.29. The altar in the ceremonial ger *of Byambadorj, a Hovd shaman now living in Ulaanbaatar, illustrates the return of the altar as the focus of religious practice in the* ger. *(Joseph Wolek, August 2000)*

tional utensil for this offering is called a *tsat-saliin halbaga*. It has nine indentations below the handle, and although many people may think this is because nine is a sacred number in Tibetan Buddhism, nine was a sacred number in Mongolia long before Buddhist times.

Twice a day, in the morning and the evening, the freshest milk of the day is thrown one, three, or nine times toward the heavens to salute the nine strong gods who live there. In addition to this morning ritual, a milk offering is made when families or friends depart on a journey, asking the spirits to guard the travelers on their journey. To end this brief journey into Mongolian culture, I raise a spoonful of milk to you.

NOTES

I must acknowledge my debt to the staff of the National Museum of Mongolian History in Ulaanbaatar–in particular Dr. B. S. Idshinnorov, Dr. U. D. Nansalmaa, Dr. D. Bumaa, Mr. B. T. Ayush, and Mr. Menes. I moved to Mongolia in July 1993 at an exciting time of long-awaited freedom. I do not know how free they would have been to discuss many of the topics I raised if I had been in Mongolia during communism. Mongolians tend to be very friendly and hospitable. My colleagues at the Museum were as excited to share their culture with me as I was to learn. One of my Mongolian language teachers, an octogenarian from western Mongolia named L. Damdinjav, taught me not only spoken Mongolian, but also a great deal about traditional

Figure 3.30. A woman sprinkles milk from a tsatsaliin halbag *to ask for healthy foals and plentiful mare's milk at the first milking of the mares ceremony, Tuv Aimag. (Paula L.W. Sabloff, 1994)*

customs. Any insights I have into traditional Mongolian culture stem from these exchanges, which are particularly valuable in light of the fact that there is a paucity of materials on Mongolia written in English. Much of the literature on "Mongolia" actually deals with Inner Mongolia, and there are great differences between this autonomous region of China and Mongolia.

1. D. Nansalmaa, "Huvtsas Hunar" (Clothing), *Halhin Ugsaatni Zui* (Ulaanbaatar: Ulsin Hevleliin Gazar, 1987), 149.

2. Terese Tse Bartholomew, "Nomadic Life,"in *Mongolia: The Legacy of Chinggis Khan* (San Francisco: The Asian Art Museum of San Francisco, 1995).

3. Martha Boyer, *Mongol Jewelry* (Copenhagen: I Kommission Hos Gyldendalske Boghandeel, Nordisk Forlag, 1952).

4. Francis Woodman Cleaves, *The Secret History of the Mongols* (Cambridge, MA: Harvard University Press, 1982), sect.1.

5. H. Nyambuu and J. Tsevegsuren, "Negen Mongol Tulgani Butets Hogjliin Ontslogooc" (The Structure and Development of a Mongolian Fireplace), *Studia Museologica* 1 (1-8) (Ulaanbaatar: Shinjleh Uhaani Academiin Hevleh Uildver, 1968).

6. Nansalmaa, "Huvtsas Hunar," 162.

7. Eliot Grady Bikales, "How to Blow-torch a Goat," *Far Eastern Economic Review* (August 22, 1996), 46.

Chapter 4

Genghis Khan, Father of Mongolian Democracy

PAULA L.W. SABLOFF

IBECAME INVOLVED with Mongolia through good luck and good friends when the country had already become an independent democracy. The more I experienced Mongolia, the more interested I became in two questions: Why did Mongolians take to democracy so easily after centuries of oppression followed by seventy years of Communist rule? And why do I feel so at home in Mongolia? In other words, what is there about Mongolians that makes an American feel that we easily understand each other?

I think these questions are very much linked together. I have been working as a cultural anthropologist in Mongolia since 1994, living many months in Ulaanbaatar and spending several weeks in the western aimag of Hovd. As an anthropologist, my job is to live the way Mongolians do, observe their behavior, ask them questions, and *listen* to what they say. As an anthropologist, I am curious about (a) how they manage different situations–how they obtain and prepare food, how they earn a living, how they educate their children, how they

relax; and (b) what do they think about the world around them–their families, their history, their government, and their place in the world.

My impression of Mongolians is that they are very much like us, for Mongolians and Americans have the same ideal of what a man should be–a rugged, independent, resourceful, self-sufficient loner. The Marlboro Man. The difference is that the Mongolian Marlboro Man is connected to a mother–to family and friends–while the American version revels in his isolation from society.

Mongolians have a wonderful sense of humor, something we Americans pride ourselves on also. I have often been with a group of Mongolians–a family, a group of friends, or people who work together–and noticed that they are always talking, telling stories, or relating what happened to them yesterday. But when they tell these stories, they always tell them in such a way that everyone gets to laugh at the end. Mongolians bond through laughter.

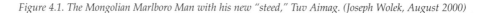

Figure 4.1. The Mongolian Marlboro Man with his new "steed," Tuv Aimag. (Joseph Wolek, August 2000)

Mongolians and Americans also share similar histories. For varying periods, we both have been underdogs fighting off powerful colonial masters to build free, democratic nations. We are both tremendously proud of our traditions of freedom and democracy.

How did independence and democratic principles take root in Mongolia so early in the world's history, and how did these ideals survive through such a brutal history? We start with Mongolia's greatest leader, Genghis Khan, although we will see that the story of Mongolian democracy really precedes him.

Many Westerners think of Genghis Khan as a marauder who burned and pillaged Europe, Asia, and Persia.[1] He was born in 1162 CE along the Onon River in present-day Hentii (Khentei) Aimag. By 1189, when he was only twenty-seven years old, he had united the Mongol peoples into an independent nation instead of separate clans and tribes. Between 1189 and 1206, he expanded Mongol territory to roughly the territory of Mongolia today. At that point, he was elected Genghis Khan of All Mongols.[2]

Figure 4.2. Mongolian herder friends laughing together at Tuv Aimag Naadam. (Joseph Wolek, August 2000)

Figure 4.3, below left. A modern portrayal of Genghis Khan by Tangadiin Mandir, historical painter and Academician of Nomadic Civilization, makes him look more Mongolian than the old Chinese portrait in Figure 1.30.

Figure 4.4, below right. Mongolian bow, arrows, and quiver in the style of those used in the time of Genghis Khan. (NMMH)

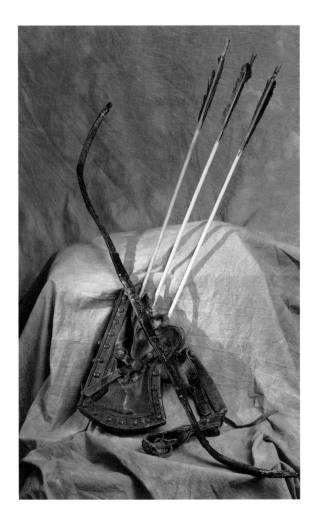

Genghis Khan's soldiers were famous for their fierceness and skill in riding and shooting arrows. Their armor and stirrups were constructed to allow maximum freedom of movement on a horse, and this enabled them to shoot arrows with deadly accuracy while riding at full gallop. They could even hit their targets when shooting backwards from a galloping horse.[3] The range of their composite bows–made of wood, sinew, and antler horn–exceeded that of European bows of the time. Genghis Khan built a military organization that enabled him to incorporate whole units of foreign soldiers, thus assuring himself a limitless number of troops for further conquest. But his real secret weapon may have been that they were eating a high-protein diet of meat, milk, and cheese while China and Europe were falling asleep on their diet of rice, pasta, and porridge! Of course these pasta-eaters were easy prey for the meat-eating Mongols!

By the time of his death in 1227, Genghis Khan had captured and controlled the Silk Roads. He had conquered all the way west through Central Asia and Russia to the Caspian Sea, south past Beijing to the Yellow River, and southwest to Persia. It is still the largest empire ever conquered under one man's rule (see Map 4, Chapter 1).

Westerners evaluating outstanding achievement during the last millennium are only now recognizing his incredible accomplishment in a positive light. Some have even awarded Genghis Khan first prize for Greatest Achievement in the Category of Conqueror.[4] Despite this revisionist view, most Westerners still see him as a terror. But Genghis Khan has a different reputation among his descendants, the people of modern Mongolia. To them, his greatness lies in the fact that he gave his people the gifts of independence and the basic principles from which they could eventually build a modern democratic state.

Please note that I am not saying that Genghis Khan actually led a democratic government. There is a big difference between establishing democratic principles and running a democratic state. While some democratic principles can exist in a society that is not democratic, a democracy cannot exist without a basic cluster of democratic principles. So Genghis Khan may be considered the father of Mongolian democracy even though he ran a

military state. After all, no one credits King John with establishing a democracy after he signed the Magna Carta, yet we trace the beginning of Western democracy to his relinquishing some authority to his noblemen. Genghis Khan preceded the Magna Carta (by nine years), and he instituted democratic principles willingly rather than under duress. In redesigning Mongolian government, he codified several key elements of democracy that became part of Mongolians' memory. Anthropologists would say that Genghis Khan established the *political culture* that is still in the minds of Mongolians today.

Political Culture

What is political culture and why is it so important to a nation? Simply put, politics is about different ways of organizing the distribution of resources. Some examples are monarchy, totalitarianism, consensus democracy, and majority-rule democracy. *Political culture* is a people's preference for one way of making decisions about how resources are distributed over another.

Alexis de Tocqueville, the Frenchman who visited the United States when it was a young democracy, characterized American political culture as guided by love of equality and individualism, civil society, a belief in the sovereignty of the people (through majority rule), and distrust of government.[5] Many would argue that the political culture he observed nearly two centuries ago is still intact today. If anything, we are at a point where we are even more distrustful of government, for our love of individualism and capitalism seems to be even more extreme than it was in the 1830s.

I went to Mongolia in 1998 to discover *Mongolian* political culture. And in the process, I stumbled across something bigger–namely, the roots of their political culture today. These roots are their traditional nomadic lifestyle and their ancient ruler, Genghis Khan.

Figure 4.5, facing. S. Zorig, leader of the 1990 Peaceful Revolution, signing autographs like a rock star. (NMMH)

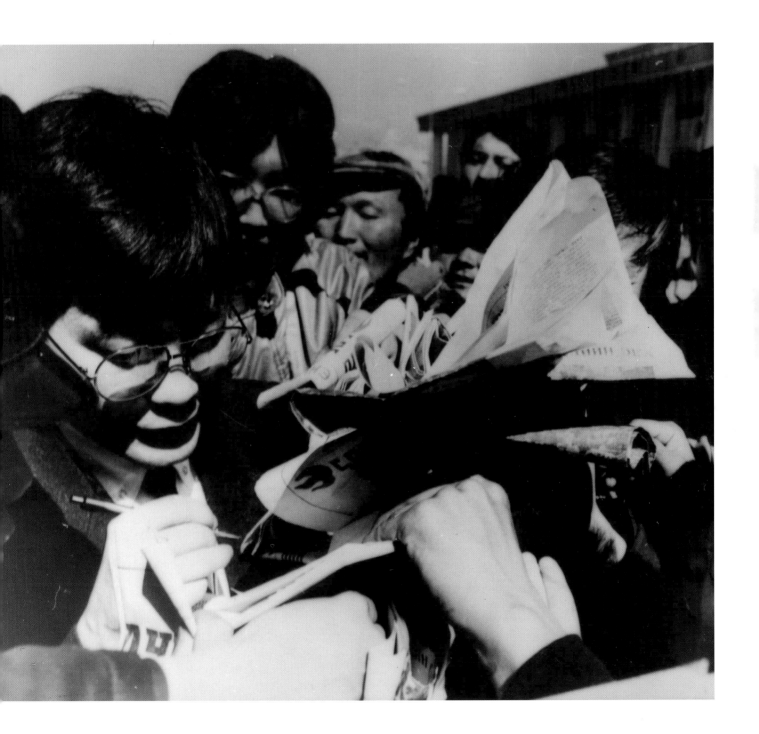

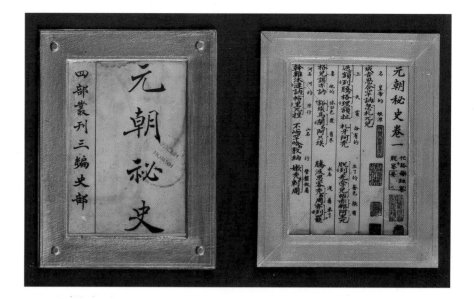

Figure 4.6.
Copy of the cover of The Secret History of the Mongols *composed in the Mongolian language but using Chinese writing. Kafarov, a Russian scholar, found it in the library of the Emperor's Palace in Beijing and published a Russian translation in 1908. (NMMH)*

Genghis Khan's Democratic Principles

The stories, legends, and history of Genghis Khan reveal certain democratic principles that Americans consider to be the core of a democracy. Political scientists have counted more than 200 definitions of democracy. The American definition is based on four pillars: participatory government, rule by law, equality under the law, and basic personal freedoms and human rights. If we examine the history of Genghis Khan through historical accounts, we can see that he established some form of all four pillars for the Mongolian people during his rule.

We know of Genghis Khan mostly through one book, *The Secret History of the Mongols*. No one knows for sure who wrote it, but several historians believe its author was Shigi-hutuhu, adopted son of Genghis Khan, which means it was probably written thirteen years after Genghis Khan's death in 1227.[6] *The Secret History* starts with the legend of the birth of the Mongol tribe and continues through Genghis Khan's successor, his son Ogedei.

Other accounts come from Rashid ad-Din, a doctor turned chief minister and historian of the court of Ilkhan Ghazan, the Mongol ruler of Persia and Iraq. This account, written at the end of the thirteenth century, was based on the official Mongolian history, the *Altan Debter* (*The Golden Notebook*), which has been lost.

Other Western writers have written about Genghis Khan from the Western, or conquered perspective.[7]

If we treat *The Secret History* as text, we can see that Genghis Khan practiced certain democratic principles, even if he did not invent them. And he provided the two key conditions necessary for establishing democratic principles.

CONDITIONS NECESSARY FOR DEMOCRACY

Independence and sovereignty

Genghis Khan's first gift to his people was to unite them into one independent nation, a nation that had the right to make its own laws. First he united the various tribes in the area (Naiman, Kereit, Tatar, Merkid) together into one big political unit, the Mongol nation. Then he fought neighboring groups such as the Tanggut and the Chinese (Chin Dynasty), freeing the Mongols from paying tribute or serving at the pleasure of foreign rulers. Eventually he conquered these groups, placing them under Mongol control. The conquest of the Chin Dynasty meant the conquest of Beijing and control of the Silk Roads.[8]

Independence and sovereignty were the first conditions for developing democratic principles. If democracy means a people rule themselves, then they cannot have a democracy if some other power makes their laws.

Figure 4.7. A copy of the "Genghis Khan Stone," a monument that starts with his name (in the upper left-hand corner) and commemorates the archery achievement of Esunkhei, son of Hasar (one of Genghis Khan's nine generals). The monument is believed to be the oldest extant text in the Uighur-Mongol script. The original is in the Hermitage Museum, St. Petersburg, Russia. (NMMH)

Literacy

Genghis Khan had one of his captives adapt the Uighur script to the Mongolian language and had his sons and officials learn to read and write in this new form. The Naiman tribe, which had ruled western Mongolia before him, had adopted the writing system of the previous rulers, the Uighur Turks. But the Naimans wrote in the Uighur language. By modifying the Uighur script to fit Mongolian sounds and words, Genghis Khan freed his people from dependency on foreign scribes and assured that his rulings would be preserved.[9]

THE PILLARS OF DEMOCRACY

Genghis Khan included some form of all four pillars of democracy in his government. Some, we know, were traditional parts of Mongolian nomadic culture, predating his rule. Others were parts of surrounding cultures. Genghis Khan contributed additional components, and he combined the various principles into one government structure, which was unique for his time.

Participatory government

Genghis Khan had several ways of including people in setting policy, although he was the one responsible for final decisions. He took the tribal tradition of electing a leader in mass assembly, a *hural* (*khural*), to the next step by having a Great Assembly (*Ih Hural*, or *Ikh*

Figure 4.8. Copies of Genghis Khan's banners of peace and war. The white horsetail banner stands for peace, and the black signifies war. (NMMH)

Khural) of Mongols meet periodically. The usual topic was the matter of war and peace, but they discussed other policy issues as well.[10]

Genghis Khan also maintained a Council of Wise Men that met with him regularly. Acting as his cabinet, they helped him think through major policy decisions. While he started his council with Mongol supporters, he eventually included men from other tribes and nations in the council.[11]

One of the four pillars of Western democracy is participatory government.[12] While true participatory democracy includes all adults–men and women, rich and poor—the Great Assembly and Council of Wise Men are good starting places for participatory government. After all, we consider ancient Athens to be the first democracy, yet only men who were not slaves could take up citizenship responsibilities and vote. Women and slaves were not allowed to participate in the democratic process.[13] Americans trace the beginning of our democracy to the notion that participatory government meant only the king and barons in England.

Mongolian participatory democracy preceded Genghis Khan; it was already part of the nomadic tradition, as the *hural* preceded Genghis Khan's *Ih Hural*. But Genghis Khan extended and regularized participatory democracy when he formalized the meetings of the Great Assembly and Council of Wise Men.

Rule by law: the beginning of equality

In 1206, Genghis Khan appointed Shigi-hutuhu to write down Genghis Khan's legal decisions as well as the rewards (titles, responsibilities, and material goods including captives) he granted his loyal followers. By establishing the rule of law, Genghis Khan lifted his people from fractious tribal groups to law-abiding citizens.

Genghis Khan also made Shigi-hutuhu the first judge. In that capacity, Shigi-hutuhu listened to disputes and transgressions of the law, imposing sentences ranging from fines to death for robbery, deception, adultery, etc. He was also made responsible for the judiciary system throughout the empire.[14]

The second pillar of democracy is rule by law. When Solon established the rule of law in ancient Athens (594 BCE),[15] he changed government from forcing people to obey the whims of a single person (king, ruler) or group of people (oligarchy) to obeying laws that apply to everyone, or at least to whole groups of people. By adopting rule by law, Genghis Khan placed the Mongol nation in the position of a fair and just society where everyone had to obey the law. However, in granting favors to his loyal followers, one of his rewards was to exempt them from punishment for up to nine transgressions.[16]

commoner could advance through the army hierarchy by virtue of merit promotions.

Genghis Khan also used the concept of meritocracy to staff his Council of Wise Men. Wise men, no matter what their birth and no matter where they came from, were welcomed into his Advisory Council.[18]

Meritocracy is a way of saying that all people are equal in a society. It is what they do that counts, not who their parents are. Equality in Western democracy really means *legal* equality (all are equal before the law), but meritocracy increases the chances that people are treated equally.[19]

2. *Equality through respect for women (and, by extension, all groups).* When Genghis Khan ruled, women in Asia and Europe were not treated as the equals of men. Their male kin usually gave them to others in marriage without their consent, and they had no formal voice in government. This was true in Genghis Khan's Mongolia also.

But *The Secret History of the Mongols* gives several examples of women making key decisions, telling Genghis Khan how to live and what to do. For example, according to the legend, Genghis Khan's ancestress, Alan Ho'a, had five sons who were constantly fighting with each other. One day she gathered them around the hearth fire and gave them each an arrow. She told them to break it, which they did with ease. Then she tied five arrows together and told them to break the bundle. None of them could. She then told her sons, "Brothers who work separately, like a single arrow shaft, can be easily broken, but brothers who stand together against the world, like a bundle of arrows, cannot be broken."[20]

When Genghis Khan was a boy, he and his half-brothers were incessantly fighting. His mother, Ho'elun, used the tale of Alan Ho'a to teach her sons the same principle of male kin standing together.[21] Genghis Khan lived by this principle all his life.

Genghis Khan's wife, Borte, was also politically important, for she warned him against a rival who was plotting against him. But most telling is the passage in *The Secret History* that first describes Borte when she is ten years old. She is described in the same words used to describe the child Temujin, Genghis Khan's birth name:

. . . he [Genghis Khan's father] saw a maiden

Figure 4.9. Artist Chimiddorj's rendition of Genghis Khan as statesman. (Ulaanbaatar, 2001)

Equality of citizens

Genghis Khan initiated the concept that all citizens are equal in two different ways.

1. *Equality through meritocracy.* When Genghis Khan built his army, he organized the soldiers into units of 10. Their leader reported to the leader of 10 units, or 100 men. The next leaders were of 1,000 and then 10,000 men (actually, the words and concept came from the ancient Hunnu). Genghis Khan appointed the leader of each unit, for he knew his men well. *The Secret History of the Mongols* tells us that Genghis Khan selected these leaders for their loyalty, ability, and bravery, not because they were of noble birth.[17] This meant that a

Figure 4.10. Statue of Genghis Khan in the national honor ger located in the courtyard of Government House, the building that houses parliament and central government offices, Ulaanbaatar. (Joseph Wolek, August 2000)

With light in her face
With fire in her eyes.[22]

In other words, Genghis Khan's father sought an intelligent and equal partner for his son, not a brainless beauty.

While these stories are not the same as giving women equality–the vote, a part of government decision making, equal pay for equal work–they set a baseline for treating women with respect, and they have the potential to lead to equal citizenship or to political equality.

This respect is borne out today. Munhtuya Altangerel, author of the first chapter, says that in Mongolian society today, mothers have a special position. They are seen as sources of wisdom, and people go to their mothers for advice. Many popular songs are about mothers. What interested Tuya when she moved to America was that we have several swear words that incorporate the word "mother." But in Mongolia, there are no swear words that include mother. She feels that American English degrades mothers whereas the Mongolian language does not.

Figure 4.11. Equality of women is illustrated in this photograph of the September 2 parade commemorating the fifty-fifth anniversary of the joint Russian-Mongolian defeat of the Japanese in World War II. (Joseph Wolek, September 2000)

Genghis Khan did not grant his people the basic human rights and freedoms that we Americans enjoy and Mongolians prize so highly. But he did allow a certain amount of *freedom of speech* or he never would have figured out who the Wise Men were!

He also championed *freedom of religion*. Although he himself practiced shamanism, he believed that the other religions of the region–Nestorian Christianity, Buddhism, Taoism, and Islam–had merit and should be tolerated. He declared that all religions should be respected and that none should be elevated above the others.[23]

Pastoral nomadism naturally encourages personal freedom. Even in Manchu times, serfs–nomads tied to a prince (a direct descendant of Genghis Khan) or to a noble–were free once they left the compound of their overlord. Although they reported to their overlord several times a year, they were free to do as they pleased in the countryside.

Freedom of religion is the third pillar of democracy, a personal freedom that is also a way of respecting differences. A democracy is based on equality of all citizens whether or not they are different from the majority. In fact, pluralism–the acceptance of differences and the ability to allow citizens of all groups to participate in government–is a hallmark of democracy.[24] Therefore Genghis Khan's insistence on religious tolerance is not only a mark of respect for human rights and freedoms but also a sign of equality among citizens.

Genghis Khan's True Legacy: Mongolians' Political Culture

These are Genghis Khan's democratic principles. *The Secret History* and historians attest to their practice during Genghis Khan's rule. But history can be found in books, dead, or it can be found living in the minds of a people. To turn history into political culture, the people alive today have to keep the past in their memory so that they can draw on it when they want. So what if Genghis Khan established democratic principles? Do his people remember these principles? Have Genghis Khan's democratic principles become part of the political culture of present-day Mongolians? These are some of the questions that inspired my research.

I returned to Mongolia in the summer of 1998 to study Mongolians' ideas about democracy. Logic would tell us that Mongolia was the least likely country to take to Western democracy. As the second-oldest Communist nation in the world, its people had been taught

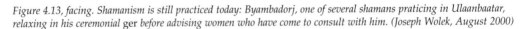

Figure 4.12, below. Bag *governors working in unison, all expressing opinions in a United Nations Development Programme workshop on democracy and market economy. (Paula L.W. Sabloff, August 1999)*

Figure 4.13, facing. Shamanism is still practiced today: Byambadorj, one of several shamans praticing in Ulaanbaatar, relaxing in his ceremonial ger *before advising women who have come to consult with him. (Joseph Wolek, August 2000)*

Communist dogma longer than most other Communist nations. And because it was totally surrounded by other Communist nations (once China became Communist in 1949), Mongolians had the least access to Western ideas for fifty years. Why would this isolated nation readily embrace Western democracy?

I believe the answer lies in people's remembrance of Genghis Khan and their nomadic lifestyle. I have shown how historians have found democratic principles in Genghis Khan's reign. But do modern Mongolians

Figure 4.14. A young Buddist monk in an Ulaanbaatar temple. (Joseph Wolek, August 2000)

know about this part of Genghis Khan? And do his principles form part of their present political culture?

In the summer of 1998, thirteen Mongolian researchers and I interviewed Mongolians about their ideas of democracy and Genghis Khan. Seven of the researchers worked in Ulaanbaatar. It was founded in 1639 with the crowning of Zanabazar as Buddhist leader of the Halh Mongols, and it moved around central Mongolia until it settled at its present site in 1855.[25] By the end of the nineteenth century, it had developed into a large center for foreign and domestic trade as well as religious (Buddhist) practice.[26] Today, almost 29 percent of

Mongolia's total population (2.4 million) lives in Ulaanbaatar.[27] Many residents are government workers or elected officials, but the real story of modern Mongolia is the incredible explosion in the number of shops and private enterprises. We watched new businesses open on center city streets every day. Most women work as well as take care of their families (more than 60 percent of women between the ages of 25 and 49 are in the work force).[28] This rich mix of people–from all over the country and from foreign countries–makes a lively city.[29]

Six other researchers interviewed people in Hovd, a town of 27,000 in a setting very simi-

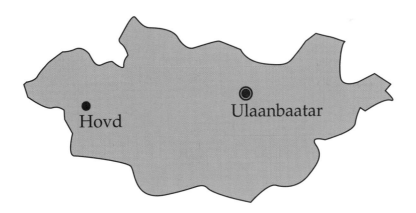

Map 6.
Mongolian Cities

Figure 4.15.
The Ulaanbaatar researchers in Tuv Aimag center: (left to right) Tsetseglen Aduuchin (Project Coordinator), Olziesehan, Chinzorig, Mongolhatan, Tsetsegjargal, Oyonga, and Enkhtuya. (Paula L.W. Sabloff, July 1998)

Figure 4.16. A painting of Ih Huree (Ulaanbaatar before the Revolution) by Jugder. (Fine Arts Museum, Ulaanbaatar, early twentieth century)

Figure 4.17, below left. Preparing a new shop in a former ground-floor apartment, Ulaanbaatar. (Joseph Wolek, August 2000)

Figure 4.18. The team of interviewers at National University of Mongolia-Hovd Branch in the office of the President: Byambadorj, Baasandorj, Bayarsuren, Gantsooj, G. Nyamdavaa (President of NUM-Hovd and co-director of the research project), and Nyamsuren. (Paula L.W. Sabloff, July 1998)

Figure 4.19, below. Hovd, Hovd Aimag. (Paula L.W. Sabloff, July 1998)

lar to the landscape of Phoenix, Arizona. Located in the eastern portion of Mongolia, Hovd differs from Ulaanbaatar in more than size. Many of the inhabitants are Kazakh Muslims or Oirad Mongols, whereas most people in Ulaanbaatar are Halh Mongols. Unlike Ulaanbaatar and its surrounding aimag, the majority of Hovd Aimag's adults are herders.

The capital of Hovd Aimag, Hovd, is now a quiet town. However, it used to be the political and economic center of western Mongolia. In Communist times, industries such as automotive repair, woodworking, and plumbing

Figure 4.20. The old Chinese theatre, Hovd. (Paula L.W. Sabloff, July 1998)

Fiigure 4.21, below. The Black Market, Hovd. (Paula L.W. Sabloff, July 1998)

Figure 4.22, facing. People living in gers along the Hovd River instead of in their apartments in the summertime. (Paula L.W. Sabloff, July 1998)

flourished, and Chinese Communist partners built a regional theatre, TV station, and junior agricultural college there. But by the time I visited in 1998, the theatre sat empty and there was no electricity to run the TV station. I never saw the factories and no one mentioned them to me. Still, I visited the active open-air market and the branch campus of the National University of Mongolia, where people could take courses in the English language and computer science along with more traditional courses such as history, geography, physics, and mathematics.

Most difficult for the inhabitants is the breakdown of the Soviet system, which means that four-story apartment buildings built by the Soviets and Chinese no longer have electricity. In 1998, cold water was pumped into the apartments once a day, just enough to fill the bathtub with water that would be siphoned off for cooking, drinking, and bathing. The old cook stoves had to be replaced with wood- or coal-burning Chinese stoves, and someone in the family had to carry the fuel up the unlit stairs to the apartment. There was no electricity to read or watch TV at night. Instead, people used battery-operated radios and flashlights or kerosene lamps. In the summer, many city-dwellers moved back to *ger*s along the Hovd River, where life was easier than apartment living under these conditions.

Figure 4.23. Everyone wants to talk about democracy. We interview nomads enjoying a Naadam picnic, Tuv Aimag. (Paula L.W. Sabloff, July 1998)

Table 4.1. Mongolians' vs. American Students' Lists of Characteristics of a Democratic Country, in order from most frequently mentioned to least frequently mentioned

Mongolian	*American*
1. Personal freedoms (of speech, religion, movement, demonstrations, pluralism, etc.) are guaranteed.	Same
2. A multi-party system drives the democratic election process and representative (participatory) government.	Rule by law prevails through the Constitution.
3. Human rights are protected.	A multi-party system drives the democratic election process
4. A free-market economy, including open competition and privatization, operates.	Capitalism/market economy organizes the economy.
5. The rule of law prevails; government, laws, and courts are just/fair.	The system of government is controlled through checks and balances.
6. Freedom of the media ("press") is guaranteed.	Individual rights are protected.
7. *Glasnost'* (openness in government and no government corruption) prevails.	Government is of/by the people
8. All are equal under the law and enjoy equal rights.	Examples: USA, ancient Greece, Rome.
9. Society is humane, democratic.	All are equal under the law; equal rights are guaranteed.

867 Mongolian citizens interviewed (402 from Hovd, 465 from Ulaanbaatar), 1998; 2,831 items listed. 20 undergraduate and graduate students interviewed at the University of Pittsburgh, 1994–all are American citizens born and raised in the United States; 149 items listed.

The project researchers in Hovd and Ulaan-baatar interviewed 867 people in the two urban centers and surrounding countryside. We worked to get voting-age citizens from all walks of life: men and women; young, middle-aged, and old; herders, government workers, business people, professionals, and students; people with no more than an eighth-grade education to people holding Ph.D.'s and pro-fessional degrees; people with different reli-gions and ethnic identities; and people who voted for different political parties in recent democratic elections (1992, 1996, 1997).[30]

We started by asking Mongolian citizens to "Please list the characteristics that make a country a democracy." Their answers are in the first column of Table 3.1. The reader will see that their list is not very different from the list made by my American students in my classes, as seen in the second column of Table 4.1.

The first item on the two lists is exactly the same, for Mongolians and American students name personal freedoms (freedom of speech,

Figure 4.24. Even young people are deeply involved in talking about democracy: Oyonga interviewing a young herder at the picnic, Tuv Aimag. (Paula L.W. Sabloff, July 1998)

Figure 4.25. G. Nyamdavaa interviewing a Kazakh businessman in his ger *while the businessman's wife listens intently, Hovd Center, Hovd Aimag. (Paula L.W. Sabloff, July 1998)*

Figure 4.26. Data crunching at National University of Mongolia—Hovd: Mongolhatan from the Ulaanbaatar campus working with Hovd computer specialists to rid our data programs of "bugs." (Paula L.W. Sabloff, August 1998)

Figure 4.26. More than twenty-three newspapers are published in Ulaanbaatar alone. (Joseph Wolek, August 2000)

religion, movement within the country) as the paramount characteristic of a democratic country. These freedoms are so important to Mongolians, who lost those rights during the Communist years. The details in the two definitions vary somewhat, for Mongolians include in their list of personal freedoms the right to demonstrate and associate with whom they choose, while the Americans name freedom of choice (freedom to make decisions for oneself) and freedom of lifestyle in addition to freedom of speech, religion, and movement. I have included pluralism, the right to freely express different opinions from the government, in this category. Mongolians name it frequently; Americans rarely do.

The second most important characteristic for Mongolians is the democratic voting process, which is the third on the Americans' list. But whereas American students put "voting" as the primary characteristic of a democracy, Mongolians specify "multi-party elections." In 1996, some Mongolians told me that all citizens voted during Communist times–they had to! They just had no choice in candidates (Mongolia was a one-party nation then). So while Americans can assume that an election means there is a choice of candidates and issues, Mongolians do not make that assump-

tion. Therefore they write "multi-party elections" rather than "voting." Perhaps the most significant aspect of voting shared by the United States and Mongolia is the peaceful transfer of power from one political party to the next.

While Mongolians list human rights as the third most frequently mentioned criterion for democratic status, Americans save this for number 6 on their list. Notice that Mongolians and Americans use different terms here. The former use the current phrase, "human rights," having heard of its value from international organizations such as the UN since they became a democratic state in 1990. Americans use the phrase, "individual rights," meaning the right to vote, to the pursuit of happiness, to trial (by jury). Indeed, it appears that Americans do not really distinguish between individual rights and personal freedoms, for they name the right to free speech and religion more than other examples.

It is almost eerie that both Mongolians and Americans name market economy and (related) capitalism as item 4. This suggests that the economic system has become linked so strongly with democracy at the turn of the twenty-first century that they are perceived as inseparable. Note also the slight difference in language. Mongolians use "market economy" while Americans use "capitalism" or "market economy."

Mongolians reserve the fifth slot for "rule by law," whereas it is the Americans' second most mentioned item. While the American students wrote the United States Constitution as a symbol of rule by law, Mongolians never name their constitution. Instead, they focus their responses on the second part of the item, namely the concern that their government and laws are just and fair.

Freedom of the media ("the press") is next on the Mongolians' list. It is also on the extended list of American students, as item 14, and so it did not fit onto the printed list. The concept, however, is very much in the minds of Americans.

The seventh item on the Mongolians' list is something that would never appear on the Americans' list: *glasnost'*. It comes from the late 1980s when the Soviet Communist Party General Secretary Gorbachev tried to save communism from self-destruction by initiating *glasnost'* (openness in government instead of the secrecy that had characterized this totalitarian regime for decades) and *perestroika*, or the restructuring of government. While neither the Soviet Union nor its only president, Gorbachev, survived, the concept of *glasnost'* did–in Mongolia as in other former Soviet territories. It suggests that the people have the right to know what their government is doing.

It is fitting that the American item in the same position on the list is 'government of/by the people,' which is our hallmark of democracy.

By the way, it is interesting that neither the Mongolians nor the Americans interviewed mentions 'government FOR the people'–the true mark of democracy. For if government does not work for the citizens, but citizens work for the government–the few in power, what is the point of having 'the people' responsible for ('of/by') government in the first place?

Mongolians and American students believe that a democratic country treats all people within its borders as equal under the law, no matter what their social, religious, or economic condition may be. This is item 8 for the Mongolians and 9 for the American students.

I can see Mongolians' pain in many items on their list, which is largely a list of freedoms they lacked during Communist times: freedom of the media, religious freedom, justice in the laws and courts, openness in government (*glasnost*). But these items are also ones that many American citizens would recognize as vital to democracy as well. Notice that none of the items on either list implies the responsibility of citizens to their government and their nation. These come later for both our Mongolian respondents and our American students.

We can summarize Table 3.1 by saying that the basic Western democratic principles are on

Figure 4.28. Suhbaatar Square, Ulaanbaatar: from Government House (Parliament) and the mausoleum of Suhbaatar and Choibalsan on the right to the Opera House and Cultural Palace on the left. Embedded in the blacktop are the tracks of tanks from previous May Day and Revolution celebrations. (Joseph Wolek, August 2000)

the Mongolian list. We can conclude from this that Mongolians define a democratic nation in ways recognizable to us. This is all the more interesting because Mongolians had been taught an entirely different definition of democracy when they were part of the Communist bloc. In the spring of 1996, I was walking toward Suhbaatar Square with Hongorzol, an English-language teacher at the National University of Mongolia. She had lived in England, studying English, and was very sophisticated. She said to me, "You know, Paula, we have been a democracy for a long time. The Russians told us we were a democracy in the 1970s and 1980s." "Really?" I replied, surprised that she would say this. "Yes," she said. "We were told that we were a democracy because we voted and we all suffered equally. Therefore, we were a democracy even in Communist times!" What Hongorzol was saying was that there are different ways of defining democracy, and 'Communist democracy' was different from Western democracy.

Western democracy is based on the notion of political democracy. To us, democracy means sharing in our own governance, taking responsibility as citizens for how laws are made and enforced. People are equal under the law. But Communist democracy is *economic* equality. People are not equal unless they are equal economically–their dignity comes from sharing what they have. This definition can be found right in Karl Marx' *Communist Manifesto*.[31] And it was used in the Soviet satellites, especially in the 1980s when people behind the Iron Curtain heard more and more about democracy in the West and wanted that kind of government also. What is interesting here is that the Mongolians' 1998 list of democratic characteristics gives strong indication that they have switched to the Western definition of democracy within eight years of gaining freedom from Soviet control. There is nothing on the Mongolian list that suggests economic equality–equal distribution of goods–is a characteristic of democracy.

If Mongolians' ideas of democracy are not linked to Communist democracy any more, are they linked to their ancestor, Genghis Khan? Or are their ideas learned from contact with the West? Many of the democratic principles laid down by Genghis Khan are also found in the minds of the Mongolians we interviewed; that can be seen by comparing the left column of Table 3.1 with the list of Genghis Khan's democratic principles as related by the historians. But is the fact that all of the principles that appear on Genghis Khan's list also appear on the modern list coincidence or causality? We probably will never know for sure. But we can ask the Mongolians what *they* think it is–coincidence or causality–and get at part of their political culture that way. And that is what we did.

Table 4.2. Mongolians' Perception of Genghis Khan's Democratic Principles, in order from most to least frequently mentioned

1. Rule by law prevailed; laws/legal system were just, fair, and strict.
2. All were equal before the law; meritocracy system prevailed.
3. Leadership (Genghis Khan) was strong, wise, and caring.
4. People revered, respected, and obeyed the government and its laws.
5. Participatory democracy existed in the Wise Men's Council and Great Assembly.
6. Personal freedoms (speech, religion), pluralism, and human rights were honored.
7. The state was strong in reputation, responsibility, power, and influence. It was just/fair.
8. Genghis Khan united different peoples into one independent nation.
   . . . .
13. The economy operated under the free-market principle.

195 Mongolian citizens interviewed; 483 items listed.

To learn what Mongolians think of Genghis Khan and his contribution to present-day Mongolia, we asked 336 Mongolians in Hovd and Ulaanbaatar: "Do you agree that in some sense there were democratic principles practiced in the time of Genghis Khan?" Two hundred eight (61.9 percent) gave Genghis Khan credit for practicing some democratic principles; 63 (18.8 percent) said no (no democratic principles may be found in the time of Genghis Khan); and 65 (19.3 percent) said they do not know.

We then asked 195 Mongolians in the two urban centers: "What democratic principles could be borrowed from Genghis Khan's time for use today?" Their answers generated the items in Table 4.2.

If we compare Table 4.2 with the description of the democratic principles that the historians attribute to Genghis Khan, we will see that the Mongolians we interviewed have the same view of Genghis Khan as the Western and Mongolian historians. It is as if our respondents had read all the history books! This may not surprise Americans or Westerners who do not know Mongolian history, but those of us who have talked with Mongolians know that

Table 4.3. Liberal Democracy Today and in the time of Genghis Khan: Respondents' Perceptions

Liberal Democracy Characteristic	Mongolians' Perceptions of Today (from Table 4.1)	Mongolians' Perceptions of Genghis Khan (from Table 4.2)
Participatory government	Multi-party election system; representative government (#2).	Early forms: Wise Men's Council, Great Assembly (#5).
Rule of law	Rule by law prevails; the laws and courts are just/fair (#3).	Laws/legal system = just, fair, strict (#1). People revered, respected, obeyed the government, laws (#4).
Equality under the law	All are equal under the law (#8).	All were equal before the law (#2).
Human rights/ personal freedoms	Personal freedoms (of speech, religion, movement, choice, etc.) are guaranteed (#1). Human rights are guaranteed (#5).	Personal freedoms (speech, religion), pluralism, and human rights were honored (#6).

Numbers in parentheses refer to item numbers from Tables 4.1 and 4.2.

Genghis Khan was barely taught in school during Communist times. In fact, he was forbidden. Younger people recall that parts of *The Secret History* were used as examples of great literature in literature class, but it was not used as historical material. Many older people report that they knew about Genghis Khan only through the stories told to them by grandparents and parents in the privacy of their homes or on the wide steppes of Mongolia.

Table 4.3 is a comparison of Tables 4.1 and 4.2, or our respondents' views of modern democracy and Genghis Khan's reign. The table shows that today's citizens credit Genghis Khan with instituting democratic principles that are very similar to the ones that they think are most important in a modern democracy. And the table is organized according to the four pillars of democracy used in the beginning of this chapter. These categories give further strength to the argument that the roots of Mongolian democracy are found in Genghis Khan's reign.

The first pillar of democracy is participatory governance. Table 4.3 illustrates the point that participatory governance may take different forms in each century (consultations with two different groups during Genghis Khan's time and democratic elections with representative government today), but the basic principle is present in both cases.

The second pillar is rule by law. Both columns place rule by law coupled with a just legal system (laws, courts, and law enforcement) toward the top. In fact, it is the most frequently mentioned item for Genghis Khan's time.

Equality under the law, the third pillar, may have been honored in the breach more often in Genghis Khan's time than it is today (the concept is an ideal that is not always attained), but it was institutionalized in Genghis Khan's time as well as today.

The fourth pillar is government protection of human rights and personal freedoms. We can see that personal freedoms are on both lists, although they are viewed slightly differ-

Figure 4.29. The author and Tuya Altangerel in a meadow in Hentii Aimag. (Jadambaa, August 2000)

ently. Our respondents write that a modern democracy guarantees personal freedoms, which include freedom of speech, religion, and movement within the nation. The respondents to the second question recognize that Genghis Khan did not grant his people the full range of personal freedoms expected today (human rights are not mentioned for his reign), but they know that he honored some of them, as fit his time.

Based on the evidence presented above, it appears that Genghis Khan, or at the very least our respondents' ideal of Genghis Khan, forms the basis for a political culture that greatly favors independence and democracy. Indeed, he is clearly an inspiration for Mongolians' embrace of the four pillars of a modern democracy. Mongolians care about the same things that we Americans care about: independence, democratic government, integrity, honesty, and all of the freedoms that we value so highly—speech, the press, and religion. Combine these values with a love of laughter and family, and we can see that we share many traits with Mongolians. It is not surprising that this American feels right at home in Mongolia.

NOTES

The research for this chapter was sponsored by the National Science Foundation and IREX. The author would like to thank the thirteen Mongolian researchers who gathered the data in the summer of 1998, especially Tsetseglen Aduuchin, who guided the entire fieldwork process, and Dr. G. Nyamdavaa, who co-directed the project in Hovd. Thanks also to Munhtuya Altangerel, Aviah Cohen, and Jennifer Kobrin for their help in the analysis.

1. Cynthia Crossen, *The Rich and How They Got That Way* (New York: Crown Business, 2000); Mike Edwards, "Genghis Khan: Lord of the Mongols," *National Geographic* 190 (6) (December 1996), 9-37.

2. The term has been translated as Universal or Ocean Ruler in Paul Ratchnevsky, *Genghis Khan: His Life and Legacy* (Oxford: Blackwell, 1991), 89.

3. Edwards, "Genghis Khan," 14.

4. Crossen, *The Rich*, 29-34.

5. Alexis de Tocqueville, *Democracy in America* (New York: Vintage, 1990), 2: 94-98, 103, 115, 287, 290.

6. Ratchnevsky, *Genghis Khan*, xiv; David Morgan, *The Mongols* (Oxford: Blackwell, 1990), 9-14.

7. Morgan, *Mongols*, 16-27; Ata-Malik Juvaini, *Genghis Khan*, trans. J.A. Boyle (Manchester: Manchester University Press, 1997).

8. Francis Woodman Cleaves, *The Secret History of the Mongols* (Cambridge, MA: Harvard University Press, 1982), sect. 139, 153-154, 189, 200; Morgan, *Mongols*, 61-69; Academy of Sciences MPR, *Information Mongolia* (Oxford: Pergamon Press, 1990), 98-101.

9. Ratchnevsky, *Genghis Khan*, 94; Cleaves, *Secret History*, sect. 124; Academy of Sciences MPR, *Information Mongolia*, 100.

10. Ratchnevsky, *Genghis Khan*, 42, 90-92, 150; Academy of Sciences MPR, *Information Mongolia*, 100.

11. Cleaves, *Secret History*, sect. 204; Academy of Sciences MPR, *Information Mongolia*, 100.

12. Participatory government as a pillar of Western democracy is derived from various authors in Sondra Meyers, ed., *Democracy is a Discussion*, 2 vols. (New London, CT: Connecticut College, 1996-1998).

13. American School of Classical Studies at Athens, *The Athenian Citizen* (Princeton: American School of Classical Studies at Athens, 1987), 4; S. E. Finer, *The History of Government from Earliest Times* (Oxford: Oxford University Press, 1999), 1: 342-343, 362; Charles K. Williams II, personal communication.

14. Morgan, *Mongols*, 96-99; Ratchnevsky, *Genghis Khan*, 95; Cleaves, *Secret History*, sect. 203, 209-223.

15. Finer, *History of Government*, 342.

16. Cleaves, *Secret History*, sect. 209-223.

17. Ratchnevsky, *Genghis Khan*, 92; Cleaves, *Secret History*, sect. 203-223.

18. Academy of Sciences MPR, *Information Mongolia*, 100.

19. Equality in Western democracy is discussed in Meyers, *Democracy*, 1:3-4, 2:27-28.

20. Cleaves, *Secret History*, sect. 6-9.

21. Ibid., sect. 77-78.

22. Ibid., sect. 62, 66, 82, 149. This phrase is only used to describe Temujin and Borte.

23. Ratchnevsky, *Genghis Khan*, 197.

24. See discussion in Meyers, *Democracy*, 2: 2, 6.

25. Alan J. K. Sanders, *Historical Dictionary of Mongolia*, Asian Historical Dictionaries, 19 (Lantham, MD: Scarecrow, 1996), 207.

26. Academy of Sciences MPR, *Information Mongolia*, 71.

27. National Statistics Office of Mongolia, *Mongolian Statistical Yearbook, 1999* (Ulaanbaatar, 2000), 26.

28. Ibid., 51.

29. See Chapter 1 for a lively description of Ulaanbaatar today.

30. Because I based the research on cognitive

anthropological methodology, I used quota sampling, being sure to have at least twenty respondents in each demographic category. Interestingly–or luckily–the demographic composition of our sample closely matched the demographic composition of the nation at large.

31. Karl Marx, "Manifesto of the Communist Party," *The Marx-Engels Reader*, 2nd ed., Robert C. Tucker, ed. (New York: Norton, 1978).

Suggested Readings

Avery, Martha. *Women of Mongolia*. Boulder, CO: Asian Art & Archaeology, 1996.

Balykov, Sandji B. *Stronger than Power: A Collection of Stories*. Occasional Papers of the Mongolia Society, no. 14. Bloomington, IN: The Mongolia Society, Inc., 1989.

Batbayar, Bat-Erdene (Baabar). *Twentieth Century Mongolia*. Translated by D.Shujar-galmaa, S. Burenbayar, H. Hulan, and N. Tuya; edited by C. Kaplonski. Cambridge: White Horse Press, 1999.

Bawden, C.R. *The Modern History of Mongolia*. London: Kegan Paul International, 1989.

Berger, Patricia, and Terese Tse Bartholomew. *Mongolia: The Legacy of Chinggis Khan*. San Francisco: Asian Art Museum of San Francisco, 1995.

Boyer, Martha. *Mongol Jewelry*. Copenhagen: I Kommission Hos Gyldendalske Boghandel, Nordisk Forlag, 1952.

Bruun, Ole, and Ole Odgaard. *Mongolia in Transition: Old Patterns, New Challenges*. Richmond, UK: Curzon Press, 1996.

Fontein, Jan. *The Dancing Demons of Mongolia*. London: Lund Humphries Publishers, 1999.

Haslund, Henning. *Men and Gods in Mongolia*. Kempton, IL: Adventures Unlimited Press, 1990.

Heissig, Walther. *A Lost Civilization: The Mongols Rediscovered*. Translated by D. J. S. Thomson. London: Thames and Hudson, 1966.

Jachid, Sechin, and Paul Hyer. *Mongolia's Culture and Society*. Boulder, CO: Westview Press, 1979.

Kahn, Paul. *The Secret History of the Mongols: The Origin of Chingis Khan*. Boston: Cheng & Tsui, 1998.

Kotkin, Stephen, and Bruce A. Elleman, eds. *Mongolia in the Twentieth Century: Landlocked and Cosmopolitan*. Armonk, NY: M.E. Sharpe, 1999.

Metternich, Hillary Roe. *Mongolian Folktales*. Boulder, CO: Avery Press, 1996.

Morgan, David. *The Mongols*. Cambridge, MA: Blackwell, 1990.

Ratchnevsky, Paul. *Genghis Khan: His Life and Legacy*. Oxford: Blackwell, 1991.

Rossabi, Morris. *Khubilai Khan: His Life and Times*. Berkeley, CA: University of California Press, 1988.

Index

market economy, 56, 61, 110, 113-14, 116. *See* capitalism
Marx, Karl, 48, 50, 115
merchants: Chinese, 8, 35-37, 39; foreign, 35, 40
meritocracy, 99, 116
Mongolian Empire, 26-28
Mongolian People's Party (MPP), 39-40
Mongolian People's Revolutionary Party (MPRP), 40, 53, 58, 60, 75
multi-party system, 5, 56, 58, 110, 113, 116

Naadam, 8, 17
Naiman(s), 25, 96, 97
New Government Policy, 36-37
nobility. *See* class system
nomadic culture/tradition, 2, 21, 24-26, 28, 47, 54, 61, 66, 94, 97-98, 104
nomads, 13, 32, 66, 78, 84, 102
noyon. See princes

ochir, 84
Ogedei, 28, 96
Oirad, 108
Onon River, 15, 93
Oold, 17
ornamentation: chatelaines, 72; headdress, 72-73; men's tool kit, 68

Paleolithic, 24
parliament, 6, 37, 56. *See* Ih Hural
participatory government, 96-98
perestroika, **4**, 56, 114
personal freedom, 6, 32, 51, 96, 102, 110, 111, 113, 116-18
pluralism, 56, 60, 102, 113. *See* personal freedom
political parties, 58, 111. *See* Mongolian People's Party (MPP), Mongolian People's Revolutionary Party (MPRP)
princes, 32, 35, 37, 39
purges (The Purges), 4, 6, 45-48, 60

Qing Dynasty, 28, 32. *See* Manchu Dynasty

resistance: to China, 37-38; to communism, 42; to Manchu rule, 35
revolution: 1911-1921, 37; 1989-1990, 6, 59
rule by law, 96, 98, 114, 110, 116-17
Russia, 53, 68: and China and Mongolia, 53; and Mongolia, 2, 6, 8, 32, 53-55

Secret History of the Mongols, 73, 96, 99, 102, 117
serfs, 32, 35, 39, 102, 130. *See albat, hamjilga, shav*
shaman/shamanism, 18, 35, 102

shav, 35
Shigi-hutuhu, 96, 98
shou, 78
Silk Roads, 28, 78, 96
socialism, 40, 42, 48-53, 55, 66
Soviet Union, 4, 40, 42, 45-48, 55, 87, 94, 114
Stalin, 40, 46, 48, 69
stove, 81, 85
stupa, 84
Suhbaatar, 38, 39
Suhbaatar Square, 6, 56, 73, 74, 115
sutra, 84
swaddling, 76

Taichuid, 25
Taij. See class system
Tatars, 26
Temujin, 26, 99
Tibetan Buddhism, 18, 29, 88, 89. *See* Buddhism
Tocqueville, Alexis de, 94
toortsog, 71
trade, foreign, 28, 29, 37, 39, 40, 42, 54, 105
treaties, 37
Tsagaan Sar, 73, 84
Tsataan, 81
tsatsaliin halbaga, 89
Tsedenbal, 53
tulga, 85. *See* See *aavin golomt*, stove, fireplace
Tumor-Ochir, 55
Turkic people, 17-18, 25
Tuv Aimag, 21, 68, 88

Uighur script, 97
Ulaanbaatar, 21-22, 32, 40, 49, 105. *See* Ih Huree
Uliastai, 38
ulzii, 68
Urga. *See* Ih Huree
USSR, 48, 49, 53. *See* Soviet Union

women's status, 99-101
World War II, 45, 48

Xianbei State, 25

Yadam, 86
Yalta Conference, 48
Yuan Dynasty, 28

Zanabazar, 105
Zorig, S., 56